NOTHING *GENERAL* ABOUT IT

NOTHING
GENERAL
ABOUT IT

HOW LOVE (AND LITHIUM) SAVED ME ON AND OFF
GENERAL HOSPITAL

MAURICE BENARD
WITH SUSAN BLACK

wm
WILLIAM MORROW
An Imprint of HarperCollins*Publishers*

HarperCollins books may be purchased for educational, business, or sales promotional use. For information, please email the Special Markets Department at SPsales@harpercollins.com.

FIRST EDITION

Designed by Elina Cohen

Library of Congress Cataloging-in-Publication Data has been applied for.

ISBN 978-0-06-297337-5

20 21 22 23 24   LSC   10 9 8 7 6 5 4 3 2 1

For my beautiful angel, Paula, and my family,
who never gave up on me, and
for anyone affected by mental illness—
don't ever give up

CONTENTS

PROLOGUE   1

CHAPTER ONE / Cruisin'   5

CHAPTER TWO / Livin' on a Prayer   29

CHAPTER THREE / Highway to Hell   37

CHAPTER FOUR / Doctor My Eyes   51

CHAPTER FIVE / Free Fallin'   56

CHAPTER SIX / God Part II   69

CHAPTER SEVEN / Welcome to the Jungle   87

CHAPTER EIGHT / Man in the Mirror   99

Contents

CHAPTER NINE / Sweet Child o' Mine   110

CHAPTER TEN / Isn't She Lovely   123

CHAPTER ELEVEN / Beautiful Boy   142

CHAPTER TWELVE / Tears in Heaven   168

CHAPTER THIRTEEN / Celluloid Heroes   182

CHAPTER FOURTEEN / God Only Knows   194

CHAPTER FIFTEEN / The Godfather Waltz   207

CHAPTER SIXTEEN / The Future's So Bright,
I Gotta Wear Shades   223

CHAPTER SEVENTEEN / Accentuate the Positive   232

ACKNOWLEDGMENTS   237

ABOUT THE AUTHORS   243

WHERE TO GO FOR HELP   245

NOTHING *GENERAL* ABOUT IT

Some twenty-seven years ago, mobster Michael "Sonny" Corinthos, Jr., appeared in the fictional city of Port Charles, New York, and took the town—and *General Hospital* fans around the world—by storm. Through the years, Sonny has survived his enemies, his wives, and himself, and fans know that there have been a *lot* of enemies, a *lot* of wives, and many personal demons.

We have that in common, me and Sonny, that battle against ourselves. Not so much the enemies and wives part—I'm grateful that I met the love of my life when I was twenty-two and eventually got to marry her in spite of the many obstacles we faced. But I'll get to that; that's a pretty wild story, too.

It's funny, because when the *General Hospital* executives created the character for me in 1993, I believed life was going to be great: Hollywood, glamour, money, fame . . . sky's the limit. But rocketing to notoriety wasn't as glamorous as people might think, and neither was what would become a decades-long love/hate relationship with Sonny, a guy who nobody else has ever played.

There wasn't even a honeymoon period on the show—only

three weeks in and I was already in serious trouble. It wasn't the kind Corinthos gets into, either. He's always caught up in mobster problems, legal issues, someone trying to take over his territory. Nobody was shooting at me or threatening my kids—I didn't even have kids yet.

Nobody was trying to rip me off or put me in jail, it was true, but I did have a credible and insidious enemy that was very dark and very lethal—it just wasn't a rival mobster in Port Charles. My enemy was worse because there was no way I could escape— I physically could not get out of harm's way because my enemy was *me*.

If your job requires that you learn twenty pages of dialogue a night, and film every single day, without multiple takes, you had better show up prepared, because in daytime TV you don't get to have bad days or sick days. Binge-watching may seem like a new thing, but that audience has always been there for daytime TV, ravenously tuning in every single day expecting to see what happens next.

Sometimes, because the show literally must go on, you just have to fake it. I had learned how to do that, to get through the anxiety, until one day when it all fell apart. That morning I got to set and couldn't remember my lines at all, but what was even more disturbing was that I could barely *move*. I was too terrified to look in the mirror, because I had no idea who or what I would see. It took everything inside me to open the door and walk out of my dressing room. I'll never forget how alone I felt, how the fear consumed me.

Beyond that, I was also hallucinating, and I don't mean that I was seeing something warm and fuzzy. I was seeing the devil and I was hearing voices—very scary voices telling me to do very bad things. I was convinced they were *real*, and nobody knew, not the producers, the other actors, or the crew. They had no clue who I was, how I was wired, or that the new guy was in a profound crisis.

How could they—I'm an actor, after all, right? I can pretend to be anyone, to feel anything, and I had gotten good at fooling myself since the same darkness had started plaguing me as a kid. So now I was in deep shit because I was broke, I needed the money to support my wife, and I couldn't lose this job.

My demons had something else in mind; they had their claws in me and I couldn't fight it because I didn't have the tools *to* fight. See, I had stopped taking my medication two years before because I felt great. I had fooled myself into the biggest lie of all, believing I didn't need lithium anymore.

Man, was I wrong.

When you have severe bipolar disorder, and you don't take your meds, you may end up chasing your wife, or, worse, threatening to kill her. You might wind up nearly ruining everything you've built for yourself. Just like Sonny, I had tried to hide from what was in front of me.

But that's the thing about mirrors, there's no way of escaping.

CHAPTER ONE

Cruisin'

I wasn't always Sonny on *General Hospital,* and I wasn't always Maurice Benard. I was born in 1963 at Children's Hospital in San Francisco, and back then my name was Mauricio Jose Morales. JFK was in the White House, Martin Luther King, Jr., had a dream to share, and both were igniting the youth to get involved with politics. No one had any inkling that the world would turn upside down later that year with the President's assassination, that MLK's and Robert F. Kennedy's would soon follow, that Vietnam would dominate TV sets for a decade, or that the Beatles were the next big thing.

My dad, Humberto Jose Morales, Sr., was a bakery superintendent at Wonder Bread, and my mom, Martha Mendez Morales, worked in the printing department at a bank. My big brother, Humberto Jose Morales, Jr., six years older than me, was named after our father, and everybody called him H.J. My dad always teased that the nurse must have given my mom the wrong baby, because my brother was the most beautiful infant in the world and I was born with big, bushy eyebrows and hair coming out of my ears.

My mother says that when I was a child my high-pitched voice and dimples were adorable, but less so was the developing strong will that often clashed with my father's. He grew up in a macho generation and was unaccustomed to showing affection. A tough guy with charisma, he attracted people's notice when he walked into a room.

He had strict rules and set a high bar, usually expressing his displeasure or anger with a belt. That's how I learned early on that everything had to be *perfect*.

When I was three, my mother bought me an expensive little suit and my father told me that I was absolutely not to get it dirty. The thing was, it was a pretty day and I could see all the other neighborhood kids playing and laughing outside. They were sliding on cardboard down the hilly sidewalk to the end of the street, so I wandered out and started playing with them, repeating the thrill ride over and over until the mothers started calling the kids in for dinner. However, when I stopped and stood up, I realized the entire backside of my pristine suit was shredded, with gaping holes in the fabric right down to my underwear. I immediately panicked and sat down on the front steps of our house, thinking I could somehow just hide it.

When my mom saw me sitting there, she came to give me a hug and kiss, but I wouldn't get up. While she didn't immediately understand, she saw how frightened I was and finally got it out of me that I was scared of what my father was going to do. She calmed me down and told me to go inside and take off the suit, and later, when my father came in, it was never mentioned.

That was a pattern in our household I'd see throughout the

years. My mother often overcompensated for my father's lack of sensitivity by being extremely caring and affectionate. I know she meant well, but she loved me to the point of being obsessive about it, always worrying about whether I was okay at any given moment.

Soon enough, I started to take on that worry. I internalized it to the point of being frightened all the time. One intense memory is being too scared to go into the elementary school on the first day of kindergarten. I refused to go inside, and instead wound up crying against a fence. It didn't help matters when another school mother, who was a stranger, tried to comfort me by offering a hug. It didn't matter to me that she was another mother—she wasn't *my* mother. I was already so anxious about being there that it scared the hell out of me.

I did eventually make it inside, and the rest of the year was less eventful. In first and second grade, I switched schools and attended Mission Delores Academy. One thing I clearly remember is how my mom used to make me take tuna sandwiches on the Wonder Bread my father brought home from the bakery. I hated those sandwiches, because the mayonnaise on the bread always made them soggy. Because she was my mom, though, and nervous I wouldn't eat at all, she had the nuns watch over me to make sure I ate the damn sandwiches.

The dislike of tuna sandwiches would last for years, but that wasn't the only big impact second grade would have on my life. That was also the year I had my first experience with a kid in class who was mentally challenged. I vividly remember watching him struggle and feeling bad for him. I thought, *If I could just trade places with him for one day, maybe he could feel my happiness.* Years later, when I told a therapist about the boy and how the experience haunted me, he pointed out that it spoke volumes about my childhood self and for it to still remain so prevalent in my mind reflected the terrible vulnerability I felt then, even if I didn't have words for it yet.

My mother tells me when I felt happy it was more intense than my brother's or my friends' happiness. It was the same with the lows—things weighed upon me too heavily. When I had a bad day, I would go into a funk, which would sometimes last for weeks. That hypersensitivity was always nipping at my heels, even as I grew up to be tough and street-smart instead of book-smart.

I was also terrified of the dark. I had a deathly aversion to the shadows and dreaded bedtime and turning out the lights. I always lay there in the dark crying, with the covers pulled over my head, unable to move. But as the fear intensified and I was certain I could hear terrible things coming to get me in the night, I would begin shaking. It never failed—I always panicked at the monsters I was certain I could see, their claws outstretched, and fled into my brother's or parents' bedroom, crawling under the sheets. Being afraid to sleep alone would last for years.

As I look back, the pieces of the puzzle seem clear: the highs, lows, and visions were symptoms of a disease I didn't even know I had.

Up until I was in third grade, we lived on Guerrero Street in the Mission District. Our apartment was a black and white walk-up flat in a colorful row of buildings and was our home during some trying days, like the time my brother gave me a ride on the back of his bike and about six guys came up and demanded he relinquish it to them. When he refused, they pulled us both off the bike and held me back while they punched him in the face. As they rode off with the bike, laughing, we ran home to show our parents his wounds.

My mother panicked when she saw H.J.'s bleeding face, swollen and bruising. As she tended to him, then checked me over, my father insisted on hearing the details. What he found out made him furious, and it was then he decided we would move away from the high crime rates of the city to a quieter life in the suburbs.

My parents wound up choosing Martinez, a small town about thirty miles outside San Francisco. In many ways my life was small, too, in a middle-class house in a safe middle-class neighborhood where everybody knew each other. My school, Hidden Valley Elementary, was a few blocks away, so I could walk there and back every day.

I liked my teacher Miss Moffett so much because she was always nice to me—and it didn't hurt that she was blond and pretty, too. I asked my mom to take me shopping so she could help me pick out the perfect gift, but I was mad when we left the store with a scarf. I didn't think that it was a nice enough gift for my favorite teacher, and wished I could present her with a beautiful necklace. At that young age, that idea of everything having to be perfect—the best—was still stuck in my head. So the next day, when I gave the scarf to Miss Moffett, I told her my mom made me give her the present, because I didn't want her to think I was responsible for giving her something less than perfect. Miss Moffett thought it was a beautiful scarf and a lovely gesture, but that, of course, was lost on me.

In Martinez my brother and I got to keep our favorite hobby of biking. Really, there was nothing better than riding our bikes around all day in our new town where my parents didn't have to worry about us encountering gangs. We still found ways to get in trouble, though. Since H.J. was older, he babysat me while Mom and Dad commuted into San Francisco together for work. I was a royal pain, annoying my big brother constantly and promising, "When I'm eighteen, I'm gonna kick your ass!" He was more passive, like my father, but I always kept provoking him until he came after me, and, like my dad, when he got angry, he got angry.

Once, when I was about ten, H.J.'s girlfriend and her sister were hanging out in the street with some of my brother's friends while H.J. mowed the lawn. As always, I was trying to be funny or cute, so every time he turned the mower at a corner, I stuck my foot out in front of it. I kept doing that and he kept telling me to cut it out and you can guess what happened—the mower ran over my foot and we all heard a terrible grinding noise.

Everyone stopped laughing as I screamed in pain and H.J. killed the motor, rushing over to pull my foot from the mower. There was blood everywhere, all over the lawn but also soaking into my mangled shoe. He left it on, wrapping my foot tightly with a towel while someone ran to get the neighbor, a friend of my dad's. He drove us to the hospital because my mom and dad were still at work, and I bled and cried all the way there. I was still crying when they carried me into the ER, where the staff put me in one of the curtained examination areas. The doctor had to cut the top of my shoe off because my foot was swollen, and once my toes were exposed, all I could see was blood covering my mutilated foot. It turns out the mower had sliced off the tops of my big toe and the second toe.

By the time my mom and dad had rushed to the hospital, there was nothing the doctors could do other than clean and bandage my foot and send me home with painkillers and a crutch. I was in shock—I was an active kid and worried this would screw up my ability to play sports. My dad was upset and my mother just wanted to make me feel better, and H.J., who felt awful, kept apologizing all the way home while my father lectured us about being irresponsible, though I was high on the pain meds and didn't hear much of what he said. After that I hobbled around on a crutch for a while and went to school wearing that cut-off shoe like a badge of honor. I was such a little jerk.

What was tough about that time was that I couldn't play or run for a while, and I loved to run. Sometimes I'd run until I couldn't breathe. Every time I did, it felt like I was escaping from something that was in pursuit—but I couldn't put my finger on exactly what it was. It would take years to find out what I needed to escape from, although the signs started early on, beginning with an anger that was always just under the surface, one that I learned to equate with my fists.

The first fistfight I remember was in third grade when I decided to go up against a bully in school, who was cruel to this other kid in our class. Every day he did something terrible, wielding his power mercilessly, and no one felt they could tell on him or do anything to stop him. I don't know if it's because I felt powerless when my father stood over me with a belt, but I couldn't stand watching this powerless kid suffer anymore, and one day I snapped and started punching that bully with everything inside me. He was big, much bigger than me, and it was probably stupid to do it, but I had to stand up to him. When the teacher heard the fight going on, she stopped it and I explained what the bully had done, so the teacher sent him to the principal's office. He was suspended, but I wasn't punished, and the class was so happy, especially the kid who had been bullied. I was a hero.

I didn't know how my parents would react, however, and I

dreaded telling them, for fear of my father's anger. I was surprised when I learned that day that my dad was old school and thought sometimes a man had to take up for himself. My mom, however, didn't want me to get hurt fighting, so I just stopped telling her when I got into an altercation—and there were plenty of those. As with that second-grade experience, I felt compelled to help the underdog without really understanding why. Sometimes I got into fights for a noble reason, but not always.

We moved again when I was in fourth grade, this time to a house on Silverlake Way. It was bigger, and was the place where my parents would stay for more than fifty years, until they moved to Southern California. I liked to watch the Giants on TV with my dad, although at the time they hadn't won a World Series since 1954 and we were always just hoping they'd get to the playoffs. I didn't just want to watch other guys get all the glory, so I decided I wanted to join a Little League team. When I did, the coach let me play center field—just like Willie Mays—which made me happy. I loved sports, and watching or playing sports was one of my favorite ways of connecting with my father.

My dad took me to my Little League games and it was exciting when my team made it all the way to the championship game. I executed a great catch and hit some good balls that night to help push my team to victory. I was thrilled to bring home a trophy to display in my room, because I always wanted to impress and please my father, even though he had that terrible physical power over me. I wanted so much to be strong like him, and as a result, I always tried hard to be perfect—so much so that my budding competitive streak would get more and more intense.

When we weren't watching baseball on TV or at a game, I usually hit baseballs in the yard for fun with my friends. My father laid down the law, repeatedly telling me not to play ball near the house, but I didn't listen, and one day I threw a curveball that shattered the living room window. I was instantly terrified of my father's wrath, so instead of telling my father the truth I made up an elaborate lie that ended with the lamp falling and breaking the windowpane. Of course, my lie made no sense, and when he found out I had defied his instructions my father was far angrier about me lying than about having to replace the window.

That meant facing his leather strap. Punishment for breaking any rule in our house was the belt, but lying was the worst offense in my dad's eyes, so those whippings were the most intense—and therefore the most dreaded. Sitting in my room, waiting, full of anxiety, was awful, followed by that long, excruciating walk from my bedroom to the living room to face my father and his belt.

When my father was mad, he would go on and on, laying into me—my mother tried to stop him and couldn't—and I wound up with welts that hurt like hell. I felt completely helpless, but worse still, the beatings fed this deep rage I recognized in myself. Unlike my father, I didn't unleash my anger at home, because I knew if I did it would get ugly with him. Instead, I seethed, and let that anger I saw in both of us simmer and build. As I got older, it was like I was a ticking time bomb ready to go off at any second.

Really, it didn't take much. When a guy started making fun of me one day in seventh grade at Valley View Junior High School, at first I ignored him. It was the seventies and I worked that whole *Saturday Night Fever* John Travolta look—psychedelic silk tops with bell-bottoms and boots—but not everybody appreciated my style, including this guy. When he came up behind me while I was opening my locker in the hall and started flicking my hair, I spun around, got right in his face, and threatened that if he did it again, he would regret it. He didn't heed my warning, so without hesitating I punched him in the face so hard it knocked him back and his nose started gushing blood all over his shirt. He put his hands to his face to try to stop the bleeding, but it continued and got all over the hallway floor. I didn't run; instead I stood there defiantly, fists clenched, ready for more, and didn't even care that I was going to get hauled to the principal's office. Needless to say, that guy didn't bother me anymore. In fact, eventually we even became friends.

H.J., unlike me, never got in brawls and always stayed clean, doing the right thing, getting good grades, and avoiding drugs, maybe because my father hit him as much as, if not more than, he hit me. While H.J. was being a good citizen, I was *not* named Most Likely to Succeed. In eighth grade I did achieve the title Biggest Flirt, a moniker I proved was warranted over and over in life.

I had learned that from my father, too, as a little boy, watching him flirt with all kinds of women, and I also became incorrigible in that way. Still, whenever I saw him at a party standing too close to or slow-dancing with a woman who was not my mother, I got uncomfortable. Deep down I knew something was not right, and the older I got and the more I saw him do it, the more it bothered me. Again, it only fueled that pent-up anger I harbored inside.

I could hear my father and my mother arguing about those women at night in their bedroom and I didn't like that my mother, who made the perfect home my father demanded, was clearly hurt by his behavior. As I got older, I also realized my father wasn't just flirting. When he went out, he did what he wanted, and sometimes that actually meant being with other women. I suppose it's no surprise that when I started dating, I dealt with my girlfriends the same way, and cheated on them. That macho attitude toward women was all I knew, and what had been modeled for me my whole life.

I also instinctively knew my mother was powerless to do other things—like stopping my dad from hitting me, even though I could tell it devastated her. This made her sad and resentful, but she didn't really feel it was her place to stop him. She had grown up in the same culture, a culture in which women didn't make, or break, the rules. So, as with the whipping, the same invisible chain kept her from giving him an ultimatum about philandering. I never asked her why she stayed and put up with this, I just thought that's the way it was supposed to be.

She told me years later that her mother instructed her that in order to be a good wife, she had to keep her husband happy, no matter what it took, and that when a man went out alone, a wife should say home and take care of the family. When my father stayed out all night drinking, my mother waited for him to come home and cooked breakfast for him without interrogation, and then he would go to bed. She and my father had met and gotten married when they were only eighteen, and they loved each other very much, despite it all. My father in many ways provided a good life for her, so she lived with it because that was all she knew.

I started up with girls around the time H.J. moved out, when I was about twelve—he had graduated from high school and started working. My mom still thought I needed supervision while my parents were at work, so a babysitter came over to babysit me occasionally. One day she asked if I knew how to give a hickey, and, of course, I wanted to prove I was the big man. I started kissing her, giving her a respectable-sized mark on her neck before she stopped me. As I look back, it seems obvious that I had some problems to sort out, but the need for physical validation won out. That need filled something inside me and was a form of self-medication I would use as a go-to many, many times.

I didn't realize anyone knew what I'd done until the babysitter's father showed up a few days later at a party my parents were throwing. I knew pretty quickly that he knew, and what's more, I knew it was *not* going to be a good scenario for me. He was a big dude, and I was sure when he took me outside he was going to hit me. But he didn't. He did, however, give me a talking to with a tone that was a clear warning.

I was scared of him and could only muster, "Yes, sir," before jumping on my bike and taking off.

My brother started dating another girl, Cory, and right after moving out, worked at a bakery. Much like my dad, he had a head for numbers and quickly developed a business plan and personal goals. Sure enough, he also married Cory and started a family without delay.

Not me. I didn't have a clear path, let alone a goal, and I wasn't interested in math or studying or good grades; my only interest in school was the social opportunities it opened up for me. Friends, parties, and girls, now, *that's* where it was at.

I also loved movies and escaping into different worlds and adventures on the big screen.

But one movie exacerbated my fear of the dark. My mother and father forbade me to see *The Exorcist*, but I disobeyed them and snuck out of the house one day to see it with some buddies. As I sat in the theater in the dark, I wished I had listened to my parents, but I wasn't going to let the guys know I had any regrets. It was almost impossible to hide my fear as the movie unfolded, and when I came home I was so rattled I refused to go to bed for fear of what I might see when I closed my eyes. Of course, I couldn't avoid sleep forever, and when I finally did drift off, I had terrible nightmares. Demons were surrounding me and I couldn't escape.

The undercurrent of good vs. evil and the battle between God and the devil in the film had burrowed its way into my subconscious. It continued to lurk even as I grew older, and fed into my sense that whatever I was running from wasn't good.

Needless to say, I didn't see any more scary movies. I did, however, love action movies, and my heroes, the guys I wanted to be like—aside from my dad—were the larger-than-life men I saw fighting bad dudes on the big screen. When I was younger, my favorites were Bruce Lee movies and *Billy Jack*, and as I got older I discovered Al Pacino and Robert De Niro.

After I saw a Bruce Lee movie for the first time, like every other kid who'd done the same, I wanted to take tae kwon do. Sure enough, my dad took me to martial arts classes every week, and when I was thirteen I competed in my first match. Although I was very good on my feet and could side kick, I was up against a seventeen-year-old who was huge, and I remember standing there looking at him and shaking with fear, desperately wishing I were bigger.

The guy looked at the referee and asked in disbelief, "You want me to fight *him*?"

My mom was in the stands and I could feel her fear as she watched us begin. When the guy kicked me in the stomach, he did it so hard that it knocked the wind out of me. The referee actually had to stop the fight to pump my chest, and my mom was so upset she came running out of the stands and hovered over him, crying, yelling, and begging God to save me.

When I finally gasped for air and sat up, I'll never forget the master sitting next to me and explaining it shouldn't have happened. But, he added, it would make me stronger.

I guess it did, because at my second tournament I won a trophy.

I went on to earn the green belt and then the red belt, but then, after three years, I stopped practicing. It would have taken another year to get a black belt, and by that time I felt I had the moves I needed.

I didn't get involved in a sport again until I tried out for the football team my freshman year at College Park High School. It seemed like such a cool-guy sport, and at the time I loved watching the 49ers on TV with my dad. I liked the quarterback, John Brodie, but the team didn't make it to the Super Bowl. I did well and made the team, the Falcons, playing defensive back, but my first clue that I wasn't going to enjoy football, other than watching it on TV, was the training. We practiced in the mud, heat, and rain and the coach had no mercy—it was horrendous, and it's also a brutal game. As a defensive back, I got hit a lot covering the wide receiver to make sure he didn't get the ball, and after all that training and getting hit, we weren't even a great team. We won maybe three games, so I decided not to play the next year because it wasn't my kind of cool after all.

By this time my father considered me a man and had stopped the whippings, but the anger and fear that accompanied them had already become a deep part of my consciousness. Whether or not I realized it, those feelings had infused my life and informed my behavior.

After school and on weekends I hung out with my close buddies Jeff Bigby, Teddy Toribio, Richard Viallanueva, Mo Pagan, and Murray Kehrlein, who were a mix of Filipino, Spanish, Mexican, and African American. I was the lone Salvadoran-Nicaraguan in the group and we proved to be a motley crew—and an inseparable one, at that. I had a particularly competitive relationship with my friend Randy Gallerin, who wanted to be a musician and thought he was cooler than anybody else, and we would vie for everything from the same cars to the same girls for years.

Once me and my buddies were old enough to drive, we found our way into trouble, and Main Street in Walnut Creek was the drag where all the action took place. Whenever we got a chance, we piled into lowriders and cruised up and down the strip with all the other carloads full of guys driving around looking at each other and talking trash—a recipe for disaster.

One time I was in my dad's Datsun 510 hanging out with Kurt and Greg Olsen. They were massive, burly guys who made us feel untouchable, so we could talk as much trash as we wanted. While we were cruising, some guys in a lowrider pulled up beside us, keeping pace for a while as everyone yelled shit back and forth. Suddenly one of them threw a beer bottle at my window, and the chase was on.

We skidded around backstreets, chasing them all the way to a parking lot, where they unexpectedly stopped and waited, idling. We idled, too, ready to jump out and throw some fists. A few tense moments passed with only the sound of the motors rumbling.

Then we heard one of them yell, "Hey, man, get the gun!"

That did it for us. We heard the word *gun* and hit the gas, squealing right out of the parking lot. Luckily, they didn't follow us. Me and my friends did a lot of things, but we were not into weapons. We liked making mischief and trouble, but we needed to be alive to do so.

In my junior year a new kid, Peter Durant, came to school and became part of my crew. Since his brother, Marco, was a professional boxer, I got hooked on the sport and bought a boxing bag for myself. I hung it in the garage, thinking it was another cool sport I could conquer. I also watched fights on TV with my dad all the time and loved Muhammad Ali like everyone else—he was the greatest because he had enough power to get respect and his speed and footwork were second to none.

One day when I was about seventeen, Peter brought his brother to my house to hang out and as I started punching the bag Marco watched for a while.

"Mauricio, you have the talent to be a professional boxer," he said. But there was a kicker. "You have to lose twenty pounds, and you'll get your nose broken."

That was that for me.

I figured I wouldn't pursue boxing, but it's lucky I learned around this time something I really liked: the sound of applause. My parents often entertained and always had plenty of tunes, drink, and food, and after everyone had been drinking and dancing awhile, my father usually gathered everyone around in a circle to have me sing Michael Jackson's ballad "Ben." The first time he did this, I wasn't so sure I wanted to, but once I saw the reaction and experienced that feeling of adoration from a crowd, I was enthusiastic. I loved the attention, and from that point on perfected my performance to elicit the maximum applause.

At these parties there was always alcohol, which proved to get me in trouble, starting at a very young age—but, surprisingly, not with my father. Lying was punishable, as was smoking or doing drugs, but alcohol . . . now, that was a different story to him. You're a man, so you drink. What was the harm in a little beer now and then? There was some harm in it, of course, like the time our family traveled to Nicaragua to visit my father's family, and I got so drunk I fell asleep in someone's house and my parents couldn't find me. When I finally showed up, I had bruises and a swollen eye from a fight I had gotten into, although I couldn't recall how it had started. I didn't get hit for being gone all night or getting drunk, because drinking was what a man grew up to do.

Less troublesome was my natural ability to dance. Turns out I had some pretty good moves. In ninth grade at a school dance, I was out on a crowded dance floor when one of the senior girls came up and started dancing with me. After we danced for a few hours, she talked me into entering a dance competition with her at school.

Instead of hanging out with the guys, she and I started religiously practicing the routine we choreographed to "Galaxy" by War at my house. For weeks we went over and over it meticulously, because I was determined to win. Competitions had started to mean too much to me and I didn't just want to win, I *needed* to win, so whenever I fell short of a goal or didn't achieve the perfection that had been engrained in me to pursue, I went into a funk.

The competition took place in the auditorium at school, filled to the rafters with students. From the moment I heard the whistles and applause from my buddies and the music started, I felt a rush. As we started moving across the floor, we executed our routine flawlessly, and when we finished, the auditorium—including the judges—erupted into thundering applause. I basked in that energy.

After the last couple danced, the judges tallied the scores and announced us as the winners, so we took home the trophy. The high from the victory was one I could get used to, even hooked on—and now we were eligible to compete against thirty other dance teams at the Concord Pavilion, a huge stadium in Concord, California, where me and my buddies attended rock concerts all the time.

To prepare for the new dance competition, my dance partner and I came up with another great routine, choreographing the steps to "Groove Line" by Heatwave, but this time there was more competition, and it was more challenging because we weren't in an intimate setting with cool lighting. This event started in the day-time and was outside in the heat in a big, stark stadium, and really only those lucky ones dancing later when the sun went down had a chance.

My mom and dad came to watch us perform, and as we were waiting to see what number we would be assigned, I started get-ting nervous.

"You okay?" my dance partner asked.

"I'm good as long as we're not first," I said.

What do you know, we were assigned number one. I had a bad feeling down in my gut.

When the emcee announced us, we made our way to the stage, where I smiled at the judges, hoping to make a connection. They were all business, so my nerves were frayed a little more. As the music started, I began to sweat profusely and missed a few steps, which threw us out of sync, and we never did recover. Maybe I had psyched myself out or let the anxiety get the better of me, but I couldn't wait to get off that stage.

That was it for dance competitions for me. However, I didn't think much of it—there were plenty of concerts and parties ahead. I figured maybe I'd find another place to perform, and I would al-ways figure out more ways to be around girls and music.

One time me and the guys were out on the strip in Walnut Creek and some girls invited us to a party, but when we walked inside everyone stared and the music stopped. It was an all-white party, and their looks screamed that we were the motley ethnic crew stumbling into the wrong place. I was wearing a black cut-off shirt with STEEL emblazoned across the front and a brown leather jacket, and among our group was Bob Hanes, a huge black guy. We were the toughest guys in school and no one at the party was happy to see us, but we helped ourselves to drinks and tried to mingle. It didn't take long for somebody to say something derogatory to Bob, and he gave me a look I had seen before, so I prepared to cover him.

"Have my back," Bob whispered to me, and I nodded; I knew the drill. Then he turned and said to me, loud enough for the room to hear, "This guy said something about me."

Raw hate spilled off the guy as he glared at Bob, and he showed absolutely no fear or remorse. "Yeah. I called your friend a nigger," he repeated, loudly, for the benefit of the crowd.

The words enraged me and I charged him before I could stop myself, and as we scuffled, I grabbed him, throwing him through the sliding glass door, which shattered.

After that, all hell broke loose. When you're fighting in a house it's a whole different ball game, because it's not a controlled environment like boxing. It's tough and it's scary, because there are many hidden dangers; you don't know what's coming at you from what direction, and you are also at a disadvantage because you don't know the lay of the land.

At some point, somebody turned off the lights and I covered myself so I wouldn't get hit in the darkness, but someone jumped me and I began punching in the dark, fighting to a surreal strobe effect as the lights kept flickering on and off. Suddenly we heard sirens screaming toward the house and my buddies all tried to get out before the cops showed up. Unfortunately, I was the last one to the door—and it slammed shut a second before I could get out. This meant the guy behind me had a chance to catch up and I had to fight him off, but finally, somehow, I got away and ran to the car, where my buddies were yelling for me to hurry and jump in. I barely made it before we screeched away, somehow evading the authorities.

Later, we decided we wanted something to eat and went to a Jack in the Box, and the minute we cruised into the parking lot we were in trouble, because a couple of big rowdy cowboys started laughing at us and taunting us. Of course we responded, but it took five of us to take care of them, and in the course of the scuffle one of my friends got hit so hard his eye swelled up like a baseball.

Late-night runs to Jack in the Box became the norm because I wanted to gain weight and get bigger, and I succeeded in gaining thirty pounds eating burgers and fries over that summer before my senior year, as well as adding a mustache to complete my groovy seventies look.

I had also finally made enough dough from jobs at Bed Bath & Beyond, the warehouse at Best Products, and Quick Mart to buy a car, so I bought a lowrider, but this wasn't just any lowrider, this was a '76 midnight-blue Monte Carlo with a custom T-top, light blue crushed velvet interior, and a stock steering wheel. I even cut the springs on the bottom of the car so it would go lower and bounce, and always took with me a liter of Coke, immediately pouring it out and filling it with beer before popping a cassette into my badass stereo system. I'd turn that baby up loud and then go cruising to pick up girls. Or pick fights.

One time we were outside with people yelling things at us and we were yelling back as usual, and when we got out of the lowrider they started threatening us. Suddenly Kurt backed away from them, which was odd, so I jumped in front of him, between him and this guy, ready to get down in the dirt.

I yelled at the guy, "Come on, man, I'll take you." The guy started toward me, but I felt Kurt grab me and pull me away.

"Let's get out of here," he said.

"What the fuck?" I asked, mad, adrenaline pumping.

"Didn't you see that?" he asked.

"See what?" I answered.

"He had an eight-inch blade hidden behind his back, man," he said.

Once again, somehow I had escaped a grave fate, but this wasn't the only time one of my friends would save my ass during a fight. Once at the drive-in seven big guys in big trucks started throwing slurs at us. I'd seen Bob mad but never as mad as he was when he pulled one of the guys out of the truck like the guy was a paper doll. All his friends jumped out of their trucks and it was on, and as I was fighting one of them, I suddenly heard, "Mauricio, look out!"

I turned in time to see a guy running straight at me, and without slowing down he punched me right in the face, knocking me back several feet, but if I hadn't turned, who knows what he would have done after he got the drop on me? By this time sirens were screaming close by and as the cops drove up and started yelling, we all dispersed in different directions, jumping the fence and running like hell.

I think back on those times, and it's a wonder I made it out alive. By telling these stories, I am by no means condoning or promoting violence. These stories are about friendship and adolescent revelry, sure, but they're also painful times to look back on. That instinct inside me was a combination of things—anger at my dad, undefined goals, and my undiagnosed condition. It's a wonder I didn't get injured more seriously in fights. It's a wonder I didn't get killed.

Although I had no clear direction, life seemed uncomplicated, but beneath the surface something was off, something ominous was simmering, and one day when a group of friends came to tell me there were six guys who expected us to fight, I suddenly couldn't budge a muscle. I stood there, silent, panicked.

It felt sickeningly familiar. Just like the little boy in the dark, under the covers, terrified of what was hiding the shadows. I didn't understand why I was so scared. It wasn't like me not to want to be the first one through the door for a fight. I was so embarrassed I was acting like such a pussy—usually it was me calling out other guys on that in a heartbeat—but now I flat-out lied and made up an excuse why I couldn't go with the guys.

My sudden anxiety, this inability to perform a normal task in my daily routine that I had done numerous times, was just another rippling undercurrent trying to warn me I was on a collision course with something terrible that would alter my life. But, as I'd done for years before, I brushed it off, pushed that feeling down somewhere inside. I made my way through high school with a new skill—lying to myself and thus creating a false reality for myself and others.

I couldn't wait to get out of school, but as the end of my senior year approached, it looked like I wasn't going to pass twelfth grade. I had copied my way through since I was little, but now girls who had always let me cheat were getting angry at me and no longer allowing it.

I wish now I had applied myself. It wasn't that I had no intelligence, I just rarely paid attention in class, but I do remember one time I actually got into an assignment involving writing an essay and then presenting it to the class verbally. I decided to write about the trip to Nicaragua when I was fourteen that had started out with an altercation with my father.

I didn't want to go, and my father was so angry that I was

complaining about the trip he hit me and then made me go on the family vacation and expected a good attitude the whole time. After all my bitching, at the end of the excursion I was sad when it was time to come back home, because I loved it and didn't want to leave. I had a great time while I was there, but one event stood out that wasn't a happy memory—in fact, it was a very dangerous encounter.

One day I was eating in a restaurant and a guy who was clearly a bully came in and started bothering me. I didn't want to fight him and told him to leave me alone, but when he wouldn't, I finally got into it with him outside the restaurant. Once again, my tae kwon do came in handy, and I tried my side kick that never failed me . . . but this time I missed. It only pissed him off more, and he grabbed me, throwing me down and slamming my head on the street. He kept slamming my skull, again and again, and as I was losing consciousness, his brother stepped in to stop the fight. When I stumbled back to my relative's house and my mom saw my condition, she took me to the hospital and immediately called the cops.

I turned in my essay and when it came time for me to read it to the class, I actually enjoyed the theatrics of re-creating the story. After all the essays were turned in, the teacher told the class one essay stood out from all the others.

I was stunned when the teacher told the whole class, "The number one essay in the class is Mauricio's. I'm giving him an A-plus."

It felt good to be acknowledged and to have accomplished it on my own, but then I went right back to doing what I always did, copying answers and other people's homework. I thought I was so cool that I was even pretty brazen about it; however, I finally got busted for cheating and the teacher embarrassed me in front of the whole class. I also flunked all my classes, and when my mother realized I wasn't going to graduate she started lobbying the principal. It wasn't the first time she had to go to the school to get me out of trouble over the years, and after her cajoling, begging, and dramatic tears, the principal finally gave in and I was allowed to attend the graduation ceremony. I think my mother probably clapped louder than anybody when I walked across the stage.

I didn't care about the diploma one bit; I just knew there was going to be one helluva party afterward, and Randy and I stayed out all night tearing it up.

CHAPTER TWO

Livin' on a Prayer

After high school, I worked at the Farmers Market bagging groceries, and drifted with no burning motivation to follow any specific path, but I did meet two guys, Jeff and Manny, who became my sidekicks, and we were the Three Musketeers, inseparable, for years.

I had hung out with Manny's uncle Mo in high school, but Manny was the most giving person I'd ever met and he was truly my best friend of all time, one hundred percent there for me in any and every way—no questions asked. Manny had dark hair, an open friendly face, and a quick smile, but we thought he was the least attractive of this trio. Jeff and I were total tens—at least in our minds, anyway. Manny's sense of humor, though, made up for his lack of looks. Jeff and I teased Manny insufferably, yet he could give as good as he got just like we all could, ribbing each other at every opportunity.

Jeff had just been discharged from the army when we met hanging out at a club; he had figured out a tactic most likely to get him out of the service because the regimented life just wasn't for him. Jeff was a pretty funny guy and a tad on the reckless side. He was almost a cliché at first glance—tall, blond, and handsome. Girls always wanted to talk to him first, and he had also worked his looks to begin modeling and eventually wanted to become a movie star.

Every weekend we dressed up in suits and went dancing in clubs in San Francisco, and in the summer the beach in Santa Cruz was our usual hangout, but no matter where we were, our pastime was the same: trying to pick up girls. One afternoon Jeff and I saw two gorgeous girls at the beach who were way out of our league. One of the girls, Kathy, was tall, with blue eyes and dark hair, and she was already modeling. I knew going out with her was a reach, but I was as cocky as I was flirty and asked her out anyway. Kathy didn't even hesitate before saying yes and we had a great time, so we started dating regularly. One day, Kathy told me I should be a model, too, and I broke out laughing, but she persisted, suggesting I shave my mustache and cut my hair differently.

"That ain't happening," I told her.

"But you get paid two hundred dollars an hour," she informed me.

That got my attention. I signed up for modeling school despite the fact that I had to shell out eight hundred bucks. I was not a tall guy, so it felt like a ridiculous idea, but I figured it was better than working at the grocery store. Plus, you didn't have to twist my arm to get me to go somewhere with tons of beautiful girls. That said, what made me think I could model at five-foot-nine is beyond me.

For the first time in my life, I had found some direction. The moment I got in front of a camera for headshots, something clicked. I'd found a way of getting attention just like the little boy who loved the applause at parties. When I looked in the mirror, I liked what I saw.

I was lucky, because the camera loved me back. Once I had my photos, I called the Grimme Agency, a powerful and respected modeling agency in San Francisco run by Jimmy Grimme, a little guy, shorter than me, who had a big personality and was like a drill sergeant. He was also one of the hottest talent scouts in the Bay Area. I was thrilled when he said he would take a meeting with me.

His first question was, "How tall are you?"

"Five-eleven," I answered.

Jimmy didn't miss a beat. "With or without heels?"

I quipped right back, "Six-two with heels."

I'll never know why, but Jimmy, who had launched the careers of models like Christy Turlington and Suzanne Somers, decided to give me a chance. The very first thing he made me do was shave my mustache.

By now, Kathy and I had broken up, but she wasn't the only thing I had left behind. A flashy red Alfa Romeo had eclipsed my beloved lowrider, and I also had a new girlfriend, Kelly, who liked my passionate nature almost as much as she liked the car. After we'd dated awhile, Kelly moved into my parents' house with me.

It lasted a couple years between us, but I was so focused on my career that I didn't have time for anything serious that could potentially shift my attention. Once I was in front of a camera, it was pretty clear I'd found my calling. It wasn't long before I considered acting.

When I met a woman named Joan Kenley, a voice coach in Oakland, I didn't know she would later go on to become the voice for voice mail around the world and the Telephone Lady on

The Simpsons. All I knew was that she was another person who saw my potential, but man, she didn't pull any punches in her critique of me when we met.

"You have what it takes but you'll never make it with that voice," she told me matter-of-factly.

The voice she was referring to was my natural tenor, the high pitch that had been adorable when I was little. The one that, coupled with my dimples and flirtatious nature, could get a girl to do whatever I wanted. Joan firmly believed that voice would only hinder me for the stage or screen, and explained that I was talking from my throat instead of my gut. Eager to do anything to further my newfound performing career goal, I took months of classes from Joan, and after I diligently practiced the vocal exercises she gave me, my voice dropped a few notches, just as she had promised.

I was also excited that Joan thought I was worthy of an introduction to a private acting coach and made an appointment with Michael Olten after her referral. He was a middle-aged white man who got right down to business; when I showed up at his apartment, he immediately wanted me to read a scene from *American Buffalo*.

"Okay, here you go," he said, handing me the sides. "It's a tough scene, but let's just see how you do with it," he said.

I was nervous because I had never done a scene before, but I started reading in a thick Brooklyn accent. "Hey, Bobby! Give me a fucking roast beef sandwich!" I yelled, and continued until I finished the scene. He sat there quietly, just staring at me.

"Okay, so you've never acted before," he said bluntly.

"No, never," I said.

He nodded, and that was it, the session was over, and I left with the impression that he hated my performance. Disappointed,

I went to see Jimmy later that day, and when I got there he smiled and slapped me on the back, because not only had Michael Olten called him, but he had told Jimmy I was going to be the next Al Pacino. That comment alone, that validation, gave me an extreme adrenaline rush, and when I left Jimmy's office that day, my mind was set; I was determined to become just that.

Of course, I took it to the extreme at first; I dressed like Pacino, talked like him, and I even faked smoking to look like him for a few weeks until I started focusing on the *craft* of the man. It didn't matter that Michael Olten's class was an hour away and would require driving to San Francisco; I would have driven two hours or as far as I had to go. It didn't matter that I had to study all the time, because I was transfixed and listened to everything Michael said and did whatever he told me to do—except when it came to one thing. He wanted me to change my name to Rick Madrid, but I thought it was a stupid name and refused. We would argue about that on and off for a while.

After a couple years, Kelly and I broke up and she moved out. When I wasn't reading scripts or obsessing over becoming the next Pacino, I drank, partied, and went from girl to girl. If the drinking had been accepted at home before, it was now clear that things were getting way out of hand, and my parents certainly didn't approve of this kind of out-of-control behavior. On top of that, my career choice wasn't exactly one in which a boy from a small town like Martinez had any chance for success—and a Nicaraguan-American boy, at that.

My brother came right out and said he didn't think I would make it as an actor, and my father felt the same way and never hesitated to be verbal about it. He was just being realistic and wanted me to have a real job just like him and my brother, but I wouldn't listen and kept right on taking classes, vowing to myself that I was going to show them and everyone else that I could make it and *be* someone.

One afternoon, while my father was watching *All My Children*, he and I had the usual disagreement over my life's goal, but it soon escalated.

"I know you'd care if I was on a soap!" I yelled, and it was as if I had suddenly stepped over an invisible line between us that I had never dared to cross before. I couldn't control my emotions or anger and I couldn't stop myself from lashing out at my father.

My father was surprised that I had raised my voice to him, not recognizing the dark edge or uncontrollable anger I displayed. He chose to remain silent instead of engaging with or correcting me, because he was uneasy, maybe even a little afraid, of this stranger in his house. This was a completely new dynamic in our relationship—me getting the last word, and neither of my parents knowing how to act around their baby boy.

My mother, though she also felt an indescribable apprehension, did anything she could to support my endeavor. She did everything from picking up photos no matter how far she had to drive to get them to typing résumés and letters, and even helping with outfits for print jobs and auditions. Whatever it took, no matter what I needed, she was always right there cheering me on.

My father may not have understood my dream and he may have questioned my path, but God bless him for helping financially. I hoped somewhere deep down that it meant my father believed in me, that acting was more than a pipe dream, that I could succeed. I wonder if maybe he was afraid of what I would become if he didn't help out at first.

The more obsessed I became, the less I slept, and the more

chaos ensued in my world. I didn't, couldn't, know it at the time, but I was experiencing a manic phase and the darkness inside me was lurking, waiting to bubble to the surface.

The diagnosis, however, was painfully elusive.

During this manic phase, I continued to party, drank more than usual, and slept with so many women I couldn't keep track. It was one big high, one reckless blur, and my mother and father felt helpless because they didn't know what to do. Frankly, I didn't, either. Somewhere inside, I knew my parents worried a lot, but I couldn't stop the manic behavior. I didn't yet know how.

During this time, I noticed a contest advertised at the mall and on the radio, Contra Costa's Most Watchable Man, which was basically a beauty contest for guys. It wasn't a soap, but I figured if I could win this, it would make my dad happy and it could be a start to get my career going. Unfortunately, I didn't win, but I did place second, and with that came eligibility to enter the San Francisco's Most Watchable Man contest. If I could win that, I'd get to the top tier, America's Most Watchable Man, and that was the pinnacle, that was where I'd gain national recognition, which would really jump-start my career and impress my father.

So I entered San Francisco's Most Watchable Man . . . and this time I won. Finally, I had gotten my dad's attention in a good way, because San Francisco was where my immigrant parents had first established a home and where I was born. Gaining public acknowledgment for an achievement in my hometown was special and sentimental for him. Of course, my mother was thrilled that her instincts to support me in my endeavor were paying off.

However, despite all the affirmation and signs of success, I had trouble believing it could last. The darkness was sucking me down into self-doubt, and it would linger there for some time.

One day in the fall of '84 Manny told me there was a hot girl working at Merry-Go-Round, a men's clothing store in the mall, and he was working up the nerve to ask her out. I was curious, so after I got yogurt the next day, I went to see what was so great about this girl.

Manny wasn't lying. He wasn't even exaggerating. The girl with the long brown hair and amazing green eyes stopped me in my tracks as she flashed a bright, genuine smile at me, her soft voice hinting at a drawl. I didn't even pretend to look at clothes.

I turned on the charm. "Hi. What's your name?"

She smiled again. "Paula."

"I'm Mauricio," I said, staring into her eyes and flashing my dimples.

Paula smiled that amazing smile again, and for the life of me I couldn't look away. There was something about this girl, and all thoughts of Manny vanished. I couldn't help myself, and before I knew it I was asking her out.

"So, Paula, when do you get off work?" I pressed. "Would you like to go out after?"

She nodded and went to wait on another customer, and I walked out exhilarated. However, only a few hours later I started once again to feel the darkness creeping into my subconscious.

I never showed up for the date. Paula waited for an hour and a half after her shift for me and was hurt that I had blown her off. I had no idea at the time that she had her own struggles and her own insecurities nagging at her. She had no way of knowing that my no-show had nothing to do with her or that the demons I was fighting were starting to win.

CHAPTER THREE

Highway to Hell

In 1985, I was still living at home with my mom and dad. I had won the San Francisco's Most Watchable Man contest, but the victory didn't have quite the impact I had anticipated. Because I'd expected more success to follow and it hadn't, I was starting to feel that I had failed. With my confidence waning, I stopped picking up women everywhere, and started seriously dating a small-town girl from Martinez named Anna, who was a quiet, pretty brunette.

Most mornings I watched *Donahue*, a popular talk show. Strangely, I had started saying, "I can read his mind," to the screen. My parents thought I was kidding, but somewhere inside, my mother knew I wasn't joking. She just didn't know what to do about it. Whenever she heard me crying in my bedroom, she tried to find out the reason, but usually nothing special had happened to warrant my malaise. She always tried to comfort me and make me feel better, but I always pushed her away.

"You need to let me go," I told her over and over. At the time I couldn't see, nor could my friends and family, that the tears were a cry for help, a loud cry, and a deeper despair was gnawing at me.

A breakdown was beginning to manifest.

Along with the mania, hallucinations began to bombard me. One night while I was shaving, I wiped my face with a towel, but when I looked at myself in the mirror again, I was bleeding profusely. I tried to wipe the blood off but there was just too much, so I ran to get bandages and more towels to soak up all the blood. As I passed a window and caught sight of my reflection, I stopped short in shock, because there was no blood anywhere. Not on my face, my clothes, or the towel I was clutching. Not a single drop.

I convinced myself that the hallucinations and growing ability to delude myself, including reading a TV host's mind, were just a result of being tired. After all, I was recuperating from a fever of 103 and had also spent days memorizing a long monologue for acting class that week. I was beat.

Something else had also started to bother me—I hadn't ever been invited to meet Anna's parents. I was sure they disapproved of me; I couldn't shake that feeling. One night I decided to just show up at Anna's house to correct that impression. Anna was surprised when she saw me at the door, and didn't invite me in, so I talked my way into the dining room to meet her mom and dad, turning on the smiles and dimples. I was funny and charming, the perfect guest—but I was totally faking it, I was acting. Inside, I was terrified, coming unglued, convinced they all thought I was a loser.

After dinner at Anna's, I went over to Jeff's and we had some weed. I finally fell asleep at his place for a few hours—the first rest I'd had in days. Terrible nightmares ensued: in every one, something was chasing me and I couldn't get away. I woke up in a cold sweat and started weeping uncontrollably, trying to refocus my mind, but I couldn't shake the disturbing images. I chalked it up to the fact that I'd recently been sick. Was I getting the flu again, or was it something worse?

I got up and ventured out to the balcony with the liter of wine I had been drinking before dozing off, and I leaned over the rail, gazing at the drop below, tempted. Before I could act on my thoughts, I was interrupted by Jeff, who had heard me moving around on the balcony and came to check on me.

"What are you doing? Why don't you come back over here, back inside?" Jeff coaxed gently, trying to break the trance.

For an interminable amount of time we stood there, me with a hand on the balcony, throwing back the rest of the wine, lured by the depths below, and Jeff slowly inching closer, preparing to grab me and get me back inside. After what probably felt like an eternity to Jeff, I agreed to retreat to the ground floor and, relieved, Jeff followed me downstairs. Before he could stop me, I ran out to the pool with my now-empty liter of wine and threw it in the water.

"I'm an alcoholic! I'm an alcoholic!" I yelled, uncontrollable. Inconsolable. I jumped into the pool with my clothes on. Jeff dove in the water after me in his full gear, too, shoes and all. "I think I'm losing my mind, Jeff," I said through my sobs.

"No, man, you're not losing your mind. You're just wound up, it'll be okay."

When I heard that, my emotions changed abruptly. "One day I'm going to make it big and we'll be sitting on the beach livin' large!" I vowed, smiling and laughing.

My mood crashed again when I realized I was behaving just like my dad—I was drinking a lot, *too much*, and it upset me. I didn't want to do the things he did that I didn't like, I didn't want to mimic his anger. Jeff noticed my body language could change markedly in an instant—my eyes went from dark to bright to dark again and my voice went from wavering to confident and then back to unsure.

Although the sudden change in my emotions threw Jeff, he managed to get me out of the pool and back inside, where he called my mom, explaining that he was concerned and she needed to come over and pick me up. When my mom arrived, I apparently walked out in a daze, unaware that I was barefoot, and when she asked me about it, I couldn't remember where I had left my shoes.

At home, I became agitated and I called Anna, asking her to come over. Once Anna got to my house, my mood switch flipped again and I suddenly, desperately wanted to go running. I took her outside and I started sprinting, pulling her along so fast she couldn't keep pace with me. Anna stumbled and I just raced ahead of her to the top of a big hill, spreading my hands to the sky.

"Soon we're going to be sitting on top of the world!" I said, laughing at the starry expanse.

Anna wasn't sure what to think, because I was acting so strange and unpredictable. She went home and I just kept running. Later that night, I started to feel feverish and found I had a temperature of 102. I didn't want to sleep because I kept having terrifying hallucinations that were so vivid I couldn't distinguish whether they were real or not. In them, I was standing over my parents, but when my father turned to face me it was really a snarling, horrifying devil. I screamed so loud my father heard the bloodcurdling cry, running into my room only to find me holding a crucifix up to shield myself.

"You're the devil! Stay away!" I said to him.

"No, Mauricio, it's me, your father, see?"

I could hear my mother calling someone on the phone and

waved the crucifix even more fervently. "Who is she talking to? Who is she calling? It had better not be the cops!" I said menacingly, racing past my father.

He ran after me downstairs to find me in the foyer violently shaking my mother as she cried. He pulled me off her as the doorbell rang, cutting into the fray. Wild-eyed, I bolted to the door, jerking it open, my mother whimpering in the background. A patrol car was parked out front and two policemen were at the door. I glared at my mother, feeling deeply betrayed.

Fortunately, one of the officers happened to be a high school classmate of mine, and when I turned on the charm and told my pal it was just a family argument, the officers believed me and left without incident. When the door closed behind them, suddenly the adrenaline that had kept me going vanished, as did the manic high, and I instantly crashed, dragging myself upstairs, crawling into bed, and falling into a deep sleep.

In the morning, my mother insisted we go to Martinez County Hospital, and because I still felt feverish and thought it was the flu, I agreed to let them take me there. My brother, H.J., met us there. Outside the hospital, I picked up a cigarette butt from the ground and leaned against a pole pretending to smoke it like James Dean. I wasn't being cute—I thought I *was* James Dean.

Everyone nearby was staring at me, along with my family, and I angrily yanked the sunglasses off my father's face, breaking them and screaming, "Why are you wearing these?"

"Because of the sun, Mauricio," he said, trying to remain calm.

"No! You don't want me to see you cry!" I yelled.

Once I had been coaxed inside, the doctor had a nurse take my blood. He told the family it could be anything from drugs to a virus in my brain, and he would have to run some tests. I got more and more anxious the longer we were there. There was a guy in a wheelchair in the waiting room as well, and I didn't like him looking at me. I thought he was trying to get in my head and steal my thoughts, so I grabbed a full water bottle and threw it at him.

"What the fuck?" the guy screamed, and got up, lunging at me in a terrifying burst of rage.

I tried to fend him off as attendants rushed to break up the scuffle, separating us and restoring calm, but the altercation had already unnerved my family. After a long wait, the doctor appeared and told us it wasn't a virus and I was drug-free, so my problem was most likely psychological, and he suggested I check into the psych ward.

"Hell, no." I flat-out refused. I did not want to go and my parents didn't want to commit me against my will, so my mother tried to explain that they would help me. I finally acquiesced, but signed my name on the forms as Rick Madrid—the bad stage name Michael Olten and I had argued about so many times.

But once I realized the doors between the main area and psych ward locked, and there was no other way out, I instantly had a change of heart. I resisted being led through the doors, so two burly male attendants had to handle me as I struggled, somehow managing to get me inside the locked area while my brother and dad accompanied them, trying to help. As the doors slammed behind me and the locks chillingly clicked into place, the sounds reverberated loudly inside my head. I fought the attendants all the way to the room, where my brother and father said they would settle me on the bed, thinking I'd stop if the attendants left; however, I continued to struggle.

"I'm the exorcist, motherfucker!" I screamed, spitting on them.

My father finally had to call the nurses in to give me a shot to sedate me, and then, mercifully, I drifted off. Some time later, I woke up and thought I had died and this was heaven and momentarily felt a surge of relief . . . maybe all this shit was over. But slowly vague muffled voices in the distance drifted into my consciousness and I realized this wasn't heaven, and I wasn't dead.

This was real and it was hell on earth.

In the bed next to mine was a bedridden old man who had clearly lived hard—he was eating his toenails. I was shocked to see him drink his own piss from the bottle meant for relieving himself. Next to him was a Mexican guy, most likely a gang member, who had so many tattoos you almost couldn't see his skin color. The guy on my left looked like he had gotten run over ten times. The tension was palpable.

Over the next few days, Manny came to see me and couldn't believe the characters surrounding me, relating everything he saw to my mother and begging her to get me out of there. She spoke with the doctors, who agreed to release me on one condition: I had to be admitted to a mental institution. I was *not* happy about that.

The nurses somehow got me in a wheelchair, which I resisted, and wheeled me out with some difficulty. As they put me in an ambulance, I became even more belligerent.

"Shut up, asshole, I'm the devil and you'll be sorry if you drive me there!" I yelled at the driver.

My mother apologized to him, but he had seen it all and told her as much. "Don't worry, I understand," the driver sympathized.

I felt powerful pushing someone's buttons, and it fueled me to strike and hurt whoever was in my line of fire.

When we arrived at the Walnut Creek Hospital, this time my family had to admit me against my will and I was put in the locked psych ward for observation. I was even angrier and fought harder than I had at the county hospital and told my parents I never wanted to see them again. My mother sobbed as I yelled at them.

The mental institution was a step up from the hospital and at least I could walk around, but I was always in a group environment in a large room, surrounded by patients. It was like being in *One Flew Over the Cuckoo's Nest*—they were all wacky, so I thought they had to be worse off than me. I stood in the bathroom on more than one occasion, staring in the mirror, confused, because I appeared the same on the outside but everything was different inside my head.

What is happening to me? I thought.

My mother and father had to work every day, but they came to visit me at night, and each time my mother got upset. It didn't help matters when I was on an aggressive jag—like ripping the curtains from the windows or throwing furniture. I probably made it worse when I asked my mother over and over to take me home, though she couldn't comply with my request, no matter how much she might have wanted to. I kept telling her they were giving me too many medications and I hated the way they made me feel. I felt hopeless, and although I couldn't see it at the time, I know my parents felt that way, too—they looked at me and wondered if this place was my future, and theirs.

Every day I defied the powers that be on any level I could, refusing to take my medication. I clenched my jaw so tight the staff couldn't administer the meds. Instead of swallowing, I hurled the pills across the room. I fought with everything inside me, clawing, spitting, whatever it took, like those street fights I had been in when I was in high school. More often than not, the staff had to sedate me in order to administer all the meds, including Haldol.

My rebellion didn't end with the pills. I also refused to engage in the group activities, and instead of playing whatever game the caretakers coordinated in the main area of the psych ward, I jumped on the counter screaming, riling up all the other people and causing a great commotion. The daily battles, the insubordination, the physical altercations all led to the same destination: strapped to a bed by my wrists, waist, and ankles in seclusion.

The worst part about this solitary confinement was the window, which rubbed in the fact that the clear blue sky and freedom were close—but I was literally shackled to a bed. When night fell, it wasn't any better, because the night felt as if it would never end, and the sounds in the darkness beyond the door frightened me just like when I was a little boy afraid of those encroaching shadows.

Anna, only eighteen at the time, couldn't handle seeing me there with all the other patients, and after a few days she stopped coming to visit. I became obsessed with escaping so we could be together again. When Manny and Jeff came to visit, they put me in a laundry bin and tried to sneak me out, but we couldn't get past the locked doors before the attendants noticed. Jeff and Manny's visitation rights were revoked as a result, but that didn't deter me one bit.

One night I convinced the night nurse I had chapped lips and needed Vaseline, but instead of using it on my lips I slathered it on my wrists, then worked on slipping them through the leather constraints that confined me to the bed. Hours passed and the rubbing made my skin painfully raw, but I finally managed to free my wrists and then I began the same slow, determined, painful assault on my leg and waist restraints. As the sun was rising, I was exhausted, and also exhilarated to find myself free, so I slipped away undetected and snatched a knife from the cafeteria. However, my escape to the outside world was thwarted when the hospital authorities discovered me and strapped me down again. In addition to the staff being instructed not to fulfill any more of my requests, I was forced to eat with plastic silverware for the rest of my stay.

After spending another long dark night in isolation, fighting the fears that always haunted me when the sun went down, I was put back into the general psych ward population. But with no visits from my girlfriend and my best friends blacklisted from entry to the premises, I was as determined as ever to get the hell out of this place. I immediately tried to convince another patient, a tall guy with a busted lip, to call my mother.

"Just say you're Dr. Hicks and Mauricio is ready to come home."

"I don't know . . ."

"Come on, I'll owe ya," I kept pressing, and, after some coaxing, I finally convinced him to do it. To my dismay, my mom didn't buy the story and instead she called the doctor, who had no idea what she was talking about—so, as hard as it was for her, she denied me freedom once again.

It wasn't long before I was back in seclusion, strapped to the bed again and, like before, determined to free myself by any means necessary. But this time there were more restraints, so after hours of rubbing my skin raw without any lubricant I only got my hands free and as the sunlight poured through the window, I heard footsteps in the hallway and I knew I was doomed. As I looked out the window at the world I didn't think I would ever be a part of again, I noticed one of the latches was loose, so I tore it off.

The only way out of this hellhole and all my problems was to slit my wrists.

Please, God, please help me, I prayed in the darkness.

Still full of despair, I held the latch over my wrist, but as it hovered there, shaking with my trembling hand, the latch suddenly, inexplicably, broke in two. It stunned me and I felt a divine presence in the room and, looking up, I was certain I could see God. Instead of slicing into my skin, I put the two halves down by my side and when I looked at them again, I realized they formed a cross. I knew, I really knew, God had been there.

And so the days dragged on. A small blessing during that time was one of the male nurses who sat with me and paid extra attention when I was distressed or gloomy.

"What's troubling you today?" he always asked.

"I don't think I can survive in here," I always said. "I don't think I'll make it out."

"Be strong," he encouraged me over and over again. I think I clung to that.

Part of my days was taken up by therapy sessions with Dr. Hicks, which did not go well. The doctor would stare at me for long periods of time, and when I didn't say anything, he would prod.

"How do you feel?"

"How do you think I feel? I feel like shit," I answered.

As the days passed, I lost track of time. Minutes stretched like hours and days blurred together, so I wasn't certain even what day it was. One afternoon my friends and family came to surprise me with a cake because my twenty-second birthday had even crept up on me without me realizing it. I felt so pathetic, with everyone trying to pretend like nothing was wrong, like they weren't eating cake in a hospital with bars on the windows and singing "Happy Birthday" to a crazy person. It was the worst birthday I'd ever had.

I began to go along with the program, and, miraculously, another week went by without me being thrown in seclusion again. I wanted to be past the barred windows and locked doors so badly, to feel the sunshine and be free. Since I was now behaving like a good citizen, I was successful in convincing the hospital authorities that I could follow the rules outside the building as well.

I also missed my running. Before the nurses finally came to escort me outside, I asked another patient to trade the leather jacket I'd been admitted to the hospital in for the guy's tennis shoes. I only had shoes with hard soles and didn't think I could run easily in them. The guy's feet were clearly way bigger than mine, but I didn't care, and I finally convinced him to make the trade.

When the locked doors separating me from the world finally opened, there was the wide outside expanse before me, and my heart beat faster as the fresh air washed over me. The nurses guided me through the doors, watching as I slowly started walking around the lawn. As they engaged in an argument over a sports game, I continued to walk, unnoticed by them, up a hill, and then before they could stop me I broke into a dead run as if my life depended on it. I ran so fast I almost lost one of the oversized shoes.

I sprinted at breakneck speed until I got to a real estate firm and asked to use the phone, calling Manny and Jeff and telling them where they could locate me. I waited and waited, and when I finally saw them coming across the way I was ecstatic, but that elation soon faded when I realized they had gotten the address wrong and passed by me. I yelled frantically at them, waving my arms, but they couldn't see me and kept speeding in the wrong direction. I ran as fast as I could after them, but I couldn't catch up, and, out of breath and disappointed, I stopped to rest at a Denny's. However, as I got inside, I realized I had nothing but the clothes on my back, not even a dollar for a soft drink or a quarter for a pay phone.

I splashed water in my mouth in the bathroom, feeling helpless, and looked at my bedraggled reflection. I had no choice but to beg for a quarter from several women I had passed on the way to the bathroom, which they were kind enough to give me. I thanked them and made my way to the pay phone to again call Jeff and Manny, who by now had gone back home when they couldn't find me.

This time, they found me sitting outside on the curb at the restaurant, but to their surprise I didn't want to go home or even eat; I just wanted to go find Anna, and succeeded in talking Manny and Jeff into driving me to her high school. The only way for me to feel good was to be with a girl, or so I thought at the time. I never seemed to remember that after I was with them, I still felt like shit. Once again, I was self-medicating—whether it was women or alcohol, it would take a long time for me to figure that out.

When I entered Anna's high school and started walking down the halls, peering in the classrooms, I was unaware of how frightening I looked. A teacher saw me and, disturbed, told the principal, who in turn was alarmed and came to ask me what I was doing. I was honest and told the principal I'd had a breakdown, was just out of a mental institution, and wanted to see my girlfriend. As the principal considered calling security, I looked through the glass into Anna's classroom and when she glanced up and saw me our eyes locked, but then she slowly turned away, as if I weren't there.

I had never felt so low.

Jeff and Manny tried to persuade me to leave, but I wanted to wait for Anna after school. I couldn't believe what had happened; I was sure it was a mistake, it had to be that Anna just didn't realize it was me. So we waited, but when Anna finally appeared outside and saw me, she immediately walked the other way. Now I was getting angry and wanted to make her understand, so I followed her, but instead of throwing her arms around me to welcome me back, she seemed uncomfortable and aloof, and asked me why I was there. I went for broke; I bared my soul and told her I had escaped to see her, and that I needed to be with her. I was speechless when she told me she didn't want to ever see me again, and I watched her walk away from me forever.

Now completely spent physically and exhausted emotionally, I finally let Manny and Jeff take me home. I was ready to argue with my parents, threatening to move out if I had to go back to that godforsaken place that hadn't helped me one bit. To my surprise, they were just relieved I was okay and my mother said the doctor thought if I wanted to be out that badly, being in a hospital wouldn't help me, and she and my father agreed. She was shocked that I looked thinner than when she had seen me last and made me sit down while she fixed me food. My father was also alarmed that I looked so gaunt.

I now tipped the scale at only 129—I had lost thirty pounds in three weeks in the hospital because I wouldn't eat. When I looked in the mirror, it was like seeing a ghost.

CHAPTER FOUR

Doctor My Eyes

The first two weeks I was home I was afraid to go to sleep, afraid of the dark and the nightmares, and afraid that I wouldn't wake up. Manny stayed at the house, sleeping on top of the covers next to me so I would feel safe and could finally drift off.

Although I had hated the confining psych ward, being by myself all day while my parents went to work was just as bad, if not worse, because I was taking the meds they gave me in the institution and they made me feel like a zombie. They also weren't working and I was in a major depression. Even the light hurt my eyes, so I never even opened the shades, let alone went outside. All alone, I found myself having conversations with God and often yelled at Him, "God, why did You do this to me? What the fuck did I do to You?"

I never got an answer.

One night I was in a bad state and called Kelly in Hawaii. "Hi, how are you?" I asked, craving comfort.

"Hi, Mauricio," she said hesitantly, "I'm good. How are you?"

"It's been bad, Kelly, I've been going through some shit."

There was another long pause on the other end before she

answered. "Yeah, I heard you had a breakdown." Before she could say anything else, I heard a guy's voice in the background asking her a question.

"Who's that?" I inquired, my heart sinking.

"That's my boyfriend."

I suddenly felt ridiculous and put on my tough everything-is-okay voice. "It was good talking to you, I gotta ago. Manny's waiting for me. We're going out."

"Me, too," she said.

When I got off the phone I went upstairs and slouched past my dad, who instantly noticed my despair and was worried.

"What's wrong, Mauricio?" he asked.

"Kelly's got a new boyfriend," I said.

"She's nothing, don't think about her," he said.

"If she's nothing, then why do I want to take a gun and blow my head off?" I asked him.

His face registered shock and he tried to calm me down. "Don't talk like that, Mauricio. Don't talk like that, you don't mean it. Everything will be okay."

Man, I wanted to believe that, but I couldn't feel any hope. My mood got progressively darker. After a few days, I finally went out and I saw a hot chick at the bar named Mandy. I recognized her from the gym where I had worked out before the whole mental institution nightmare, and it was clear every other guy in the place was looking at her, too. I kept looking at her and she kept looking at me until finally she came up to me and we started drinking, and we were still drinking together when the joint closed down.

After we left the bar, she drove me to a park in her big-ass Cadillac and we jumped over the fence, sitting on lounge chairs by a big pool. When we began making out, I started to forget about everything else that was going wrong; all the dark thoughts in my head faded. After we had messed around a while, we jumped the fence again and I asked her to let me drive her car even though I was wasted—I should never have gotten behind that wheel, but back then I didn't think about things like that. I wasn't driving, I was *weaving*. We heard sirens and saw red lights flashing in the rearview, so I slowly pulled over to what I thought was the side of the highway. When the cop asked me to get out of the car, however, I realized it was actually parked closer to the middle of the road, and when he asked me to spell *California*, try as I might, I couldn't. It took all my effort but I couldn't even stand up straight, let alone get from point A to point B without falling down to walk a straight line as instructed. Mandy explained to the cop that it was her fault for letting me drive and asked if she could just drive me home, but instead the cop cuffed me and took me to jail. I was put in a cell alone to wait. And wait.

I was supposed to go to Disneyland in the morning with Manny and my mom and dad, and I was certain they weren't going to be happy about this wrinkle. Meanwhile, I had to appear in night court before a judge that was not sympathetic to my plea that I would never do it again, and I was then sentenced to several days of community service. I also had to go to class and watch a movie about drunk driving, but the worst part of all of it was losing my license for a while.

At six in the morning my mom and dad showed up with Manny in tow and the paperwork was processed for my release. My dad was furious, and not only that, but the whole reason I had hooked up with Mandy in the first place was to shake my despair—and it hadn't worked. I was coming to understand that sex and alcohol weren't making me happier, they were just changing the highs and lows I experienced. So me and my hangover went right from the jail to Disneyland and I've never been so miserable in my life waiting in the long lines in the heat.

When I showed up a few days later to put in my hours for community service I was not prepared for the dirty, hard physical labor in store for me. Sweating and cursing, I picked up trash and debris along the highway for hours while people stopped and stared, passing judgment of their own. Even my buddies drove by and made fun of me, which didn't help. I began spiraling downward even more.

My parents were afraid I was suicidal and didn't want me to be alone for hours on end, so they decided to get me to reconnect with something I loved—acting. Mom looked around, found the Drama Studio London at Berkeley, and signed me up for a three-month course that was eight hours a day, five days a week. It was brutal because even though I was still in a major depression I had to do voice, singing, and acting assignments in front of forty people. I could hardly get myself out of the house but somehow I got through my classes. I gave my performances, including a tough monologue, and received a diploma.

After that experience, I started venturing from the house again and began going to the mall for a yogurt, then like clockwork walking up and down the rows of stores, trying to ease back into the world and get my head right. It's amazing to think about it now, and hard to believe, but I had by that time been out of the hospital for a few months with no formal diagnosis. I was just wandering, relying on my own devices.

Finally my parents decided I needed to go see a psychiatrist. Even though I was sure it was pointless, my mother finally got me to agree to attending at least one session. For such a random entry into my life, the guy they picked, Dr. Noonan, could not have been more laser-perfect for me. He was a small Asian man who spoke very softly and rarely looked at me, focusing instead on the paper and pen as he wrote down notes. It was an instant connection, in part because he had a presence that made me feel safe for the first time in a long time. Unlike during my experience in the mental institution, I started talking to Dr. Noonan and couldn't stop.

I told him everything that had happened, how depressed I was, the events leading up to my incarceration in the mental institution, and that being there hadn't helped. I told him I had entertained suicide and had seen God and God had talked to me. I told him the devil talked to me sometimes, too.

After listening to me for a while, he was convinced I was bipolar and wrote out my diagnosis. No one had been able to relieve my misery so far, no one had figured out why I was broken, but Dr. Noonan was so sure of himself. I had a chemical imbalance in my brain and there was medicine I could take to even that out and keep me on an even keel. It was such a relief to know that my illness had a name and that there seemed to be a way to control my symptoms.

Dr. Noonan prescribed lithium, a heavy-duty drug for those at the high end of the bipolar disorder spectrum—in my case, it was a miracle drug. On lithium, I could function and I didn't experience harmful side effects. In addition to the new drug, I saw Dr. Noonan once a week for a while and it was like I had found the missing piece of a mysterious puzzle I had been trying to solve for years. It's true that lithium saved my life—but so did Dr. Noonan.

CHAPTER FIVE

Free Fallin'

Now that this piece had fallen into place, the universe seemed to open up and send possibility, instead of more inertia, my way. It started with the America's Most Watchable Man contest. I had automatically been entered by virtue of winning the San Francisco's Most Watchable Man contest, but the original date of the contest—which precluded my participation because I was locked up in the mental institution—had been postponed until October for some unknown reason. Just like with my diagnosis, fate had seemed to step in.

Finally, for the first time in a while, I felt capable of really *wanting* something. And I wanted to win more than anything. Manny and my parents attended the award ceremony with me, and as we waited for the winner to be announced, they were all more nervous than I was. My father chain-smoked, drinking his way through multiple cocktails, until finally the presenter brought the envelope containing the winner's name to the podium.

"And the next America's Most Watchable Man is . . . Mauricio Morales." The words rang in the air. I was in shock for a moment—

it felt like a huge weight had been lifted off me. I needed a win, and this was the first step in bringing back my confidence.

I kept up my usual routines, but with a little more swagger. Even walking around the mall eating my usual yogurt, I felt more confident about my future.

It was about a month later, while I was doing just that, that I saw a pretty girl whose face I couldn't have forgotten. It was Paula, the beautiful girl I had asked out and blown off all in the same day a year ago. Even though I had stood her up, that same strong inexplicable force was pulling me back into the store. Since I was walking in as a potential customer, I figured she wouldn't be vindictive, so I nervously entered the store, and as I did Paula looked up and flashed me that same amazing smile.

That surprised me. I wanted to be straight with her, not bullshit her about why I had never shown up after her shift that night a year ago. I didn't even say hello, instead I just dove right in. "I'm really sorry I stood you up," I said.

"It's okay." She smiled without a trace of anger, and I believed her.

I panicked a little bit then. "My friend Manny told me you were only sixteen," I said, feeling like I had to fudge an explanation. How could I dare admit what was really going on—that I had slept with over twenty different women, won two male beauty contests, and had a nervous breakdown in the months since I first saw her? She'd bolt.

"I was, but guess what, now I'm seventeen," she teased.

"Can I make it up to you?" I smiled, trying to melt any hesitation she might have with my dimples.

She nodded shyly.

"Would you come over to my place?" I asked.

She searched my face a beat. I didn't know it then, but Paula didn't date boys from her high school. She didn't really have any friends and no one knew anything about her because family drama and problems at home consumed her life.

Paula told me months later she had seen a handsome guy walking around the mall every day eating yogurt but she never dreamed I would ask her out, stand her up, then a year later show up again. She thought when I did maybe for once something happy could transpire for the good girl who was trapped in a bad situation at home. She also thought I couldn't bail this time if we were at my house.

As we drove up, I neglected to tell her my parents owned the house. Since they were not home, Paula just assumed it was mine and was duly impressed. Once we were inside, she just looked around in awe. It seemed like a mansion to her, like something out of a magazine, with everything perfect and everything in its place.

From the start, it was so easy to talk to Paula, really talk, because I could just be myself with her. What I didn't know was that not only was she shy, but Paula didn't drink, and had only sipped alcohol a few times in her life, but never on a date. She had also never kissed on the first date and she rarely had second dates. As we talked, I handed her a glass of wine, and she was thrown into a quandary because she was far too shy to say no to the drink. She later told me there was also more to it than that, because she was attracted to me and felt a strong connection that she had never felt with anyone else. It was probably a combination of that attraction, feeling so at ease with me, and the wine loosening her usual control over things, that changed the course of our evening, and for the first time Paula kissed a guy on the first date.

We went out a few more times and usually I picked Paula up at the high school—I was the older man, driving a lime-green Volkswagen Rabbit, because by now I had lost the Alfa Romeo as I was unable to make the car payments. Every time I cruised into the parking lot, teachers gave me the evil eye and parents stared. The other girls didn't know the shy loner girl they had passed a million times in the hallway, but were surprised because I was dark and mysterious and already out of school.

Whenever we hung out, Paula never talked about her family, so when I finally pressed her about it, she explained that her father hadn't been around her whole life and she lived with her mom— but then quickly changed the subject. I didn't know anything about her family, but I did know that Paula was beautiful even if she didn't realize it herself, she was a good girl, with a good heart, and although she was reserved with people, she was a friend to all animals.

That was important to me, because I also had a thing for animals and my whole childhood I was always asking if I could bring one home and keep it. I had brought home so many pets, including a beautiful baby jackrabbit with big ears I'd found under a board once when I was snake-hunting, who I trained to jump on the bed. I also had a parakeet that I trained to come to me when I said, "Fly!" as well as a parrot named Paco and lizards and iguanas. I really wanted a raccoon, but that's where my dad drew the line, so I never got one of those.

Little did I know, but one day this woman who loved animals more than I did would be my wife and we would have a whole menagerie of creatures at home. At the time I just thought since Paula was always rescuing animals, maybe she would rescue me.

No matter how many times I suggested it, Paula never wanted me to pick her up or drop her off at her house; instead, she always got out at the corner and stood there until I drove away, and each time I watched her in the rearview mirror, waving at me until I was gone. One day, however, I decided to just go over to her house and show up unexpectedly. How bad could it be? She wouldn't be the first girl whose parents disapproved of me and, I thought, probably wouldn't be the last. I always managed to charm the parents and I could charm her mother, too, so I drove over and knocked on the door and a heavyset lady with dark circles under her eyes, no teeth, and a heavy Texas twang opened it.

"Help you?" she looked me up and down.

For a moment I just stared and thought maybe I was at the wrong house. "Are you Paula's mother?" I queried, and the woman stared suspiciously as suddenly I saw Paula scurry out of the bathroom behind her and disappear into the back of the house, embarrassed. "It's nice to meet you, I'm Mauricio," I said, determined to get in the house.

Paula's mother reluctantly invited me inside, and as I looked around I saw what seemed like fifty people hanging out, crammed into the dimly lit interior of the dirty, crowded two-bedroom, one-bathroom house. Needles, spoons, and all sorts of drug paraphernalia were scattered on the floor, tables, counters, and the furniture was occupied by seemingly high inhabitants. I went to the hallway and talked to Paula through the bathroom door until I finally managed to coax her out to my car, where we sat in silence for a few moments.

"Now you know," she whispered. For the first time, Paula's story spilled out. Paula's mother was a drug addict, and when her mother wasn't demoralizing Paula or beating her younger brother, John, Paula had watched her overdose many times on heroin. Her older sister, Stephanie, also lived there with her newborn baby,

Vanessa, and there were never less than ten other people living there at any given time. Paula was torn; she knew she was living in a bad situation and desperately wanted to leave, but she also wanted to stay and protect her siblings. I listened, but to be honest, it threw me. I'd had no idea, and I felt bad for Paula, but it was a bit too much for me to handle because I was still pretty fragile inside. As much as I wished I could've handled it differently, what I did instead was continue to go out with other girls.

Then I heard that Paula had gone out with another guy—my friend Randy. He had asked her out and she'd accompanied him to a big Halloween costume party dressed as a sexy cat. I, of course, heard about it from my friends and wasn't happy about it at all, and the more I thought about it, the more it bothered me, and I started to wonder, *Why does it bug me so much, Randy competing for this girl?* After stewing for a few days, unable to shake thinking about Paula, it dawned on me that maybe this wasn't about Randy, maybe I really did like Paula more than I was willing to admit. I started taking Paula out regularly after that and she stopped seeing other guys, even though I still went out with other girls occasionally. Paula told me later that she liked me a lot but since I clearly wanted my freedom, when another guy asked her out, she accepted; however, she'd had no idea it was a friend of mine from high school or she would never have said yes. I believed her, because Paula was different than any girl I had ever known, she wasn't the type to play games.

Not long after, Paula and I went to a party with my parents and it would be the beginning of one of many episodes that would really test how much she cared about me. There were a lot of people having a good time talking, drinking, and a few were engrossed in a Jimmy Stewart movie playing on TV. My father was drinking and flirting like he usually did, and when I confronted him about his alcoholic tendency, a loud argument ensued; however, it wasn't an ordinary argument, it was unusual because during the course of the heated exchange, my speech became affected and my father watched as I seemed to transform into Jimmy Stewart in front of his eyes. Everyone thought I was doing an impersonation, except my mother, who recognized something was terribly wrong.

The next day, as I sat eating with my parents and Paula, my tongue started to swell and burst out of my mouth while the orange juice I was drinking started gushing out, dripping down my entire body. It was scary because I had no control over my tongue and thought I was possessed. Paula was terrified, too. Although anyone else would have cut and run, that didn't even occur to her; she'd already seen so much in her own life.

I was convinced I needed an exorcism, but my parents and Paula took me to the emergency room, where the doctors immediately determined I was not possessed and, in fact, had an earthly scientific explanation—I was having an allergic reaction. My mother had realized the past couple of weeks were probably another manic episode and asked for a prescription to calm me, so the doctor prescribed Norpramin and Haldol. I had taken Haldol the day earlier for anxiety.

But, in a paranoid state, I was not making much sense and, still sure something more was going on, insisted on stopping at a church near my school on the way home from the hospital. Unfortunately, the church was locked, but I refused to leave and got more and more agitated as I told Paula and my mother I absolutely had to talk to a priest. They agreed to stay and help me get inside the church, checking doors and windows for an unlocked entry until finally the monsignor came out to see what was going on. Paula explained the emotional distress I was exhibiting and the monsignor took pity and let us in but warned us not to approach the altar or the night alarm would trigger. The monsignor left us praying in a pew and I started crying for a while, but when I finally looked up at the crucifix hanging from the wall—encased with blood and thorns—and gazed into Jesus's face, I had an overpowering sensation that God wanted to tell me something.

Although the monsignor had warned us about the alarm, I was so drawn to the altar I couldn't stay in the pew as directed and I had to have a conversation with God to confess my sins and hear what He had to tell me. The monsignor returned to see me standing at the altar reaching out to Jesus, but miraculously the alarm never went off. I was convinced God was present there with me and unburdened my soul, and once I did, I felt the weight and darkness lift from my shoulders.

After this episode, I stopped taking everything but the lithium and the doctor adjusted the dose for it because I clearly needed more to keep balanced.

Once that happened, things seemed to return to normal but another drama would unfold, only this time it wouldn't be mine. A few weeks later, I came home to find Paula crying at the table with my mother and relating the terrible events that had brought her to our house, starting with the heroin binge her mom had been on for three days. Her mother had overdosed before, and this time, when Paula thought she had overdosed again and tried to revive her, her mother started going off on her terrified daughter. Paula ran out of the house to find a pay phone to call me because she just wanted to get away from the abuse and chaos, but I wasn't home. My mom, who picked up, brought Paula home to our house and told her she should spend the night. Paula, ever the good girl, called her mother to tell her where she was and that she was staying over. Her mother immediately started screaming and ranting on the phone in a rage.

"Don't you dare! You think you're better than we are? If you stay, don't ever come home!" she threatened.

Before I could say a word, my mother announced that Paula was staying with us as long as she wanted, because we had plenty of room, since my brother H.J. had moved out. I didn't have the heart to tell her she couldn't stay, but when I complained to my mother later that I didn't want a girlfriend and to be tied down, she looked at me matter-of-factly.

"Hijo, I am not bringing you a woman, I am giving Paula an escape from her dangerous situation," she explained, and that was that. Paula moved in that night and never went back.

Living under the same roof with Paula was different than it had been with Kelly, because Paula was different. We had a connection and bond I hadn't really felt with anyone else, but I wouldn't admit it to myself and wasn't even conscious of the magnitude of it yet. She needed a safe home, but I was only twenty-two, had just come out of a nervous breakdown and hadn't yet healed, so I could hardly figure out my own way, let alone one for a girl with her own problems. I didn't want Paula to misunderstand and get hurt, so we talked about it and set some boundaries. I was honest with her and told her I wasn't ready to settle down and this wasn't yet exclusive.

It was a complicated situation and none of us had an easy time figuring out how to deal with it. Paula had no expectations; she needed a place to live and was willing to let me do my own thing when I wanted to. Still, it was an unconventional relationship and jealousy was bound to resurface. There's no way to sugarcoat it—I went out and did what I wanted, whenever I wanted, with whomever I wanted. I even hooked up with girls in acting class, and I didn't make it easy for Paula on any level. It was hard for her, and she had nowhere else to go, but at the time I was more focused on what I wanted than on what she needed.

The sound she hated most was the garage door opening, because our room was over the garage, and at night, when I went out drinking, she would lie in bed and wait into the wee hours for the garage door rumble to signal that I was back home. When I came home, more often than not I'd had too much to drink and wanted to be with Paula. Paula could always smell the liquor on my skin—and whoever it was I had already been with that night—even though she had no idea where I'd been or who had caught my eye.

But, like my own mother, Paula didn't say anything, because she was intent on being good and doing everything my mother and father or I expected of her. She went to high school all day, then worked and came home and cooked dinner for the family, and after the meal she would go to my room and if I was gone, study or count the minutes until she heard the garage door open to know I had gotten home. She helped my mother and father clean the house, and she kept our room tidy and neat, and thought as long as she obeyed my parents and did what she was supposed to do, she would be able to stay.

I had no clue what she was going through because I didn't want to know; like my dad, I wanted to do my thing and thought the world revolved around me. I didn't know what—if anything—our future could hold, and I wasn't planning my life around Paula. In fact, I was convinced I was going to move to Los Angeles with Manny and Jeff. I hadn't even invited her along to Hawaii with me on the trip I had won for becoming America's Most Watchable

Man. Instead, I took Manny with me first-class, all expenses paid, to the island where my ex-girlfriend, Kelly, lived. I was unaware or too selfish to understand how much it hurt Paula for me to leave her at home, while going on this very public trip.

The trip included a promotional stunt, a contest in which one person would win a date with me. The event was a throwback to the old TV show *The Dating Game* where the bachelor sat on one side of a wall and interested ladies sat on the other side answering questions, and the winner won a date with the bachelor. I wouldn't be able to see the women, so that's where Manny came in; I needed Manny's help to pick out the best-looking girl. I had not seen Kelly since we had broken up, but once I was in Waikiki, I decided to call her for old times' sake and she took the call but said she was working and sent a friend of hers to show us around. The friend also took part in helping me with the contest, sitting in the audience where she could see the girls, and signaling to Manny, who was watching her from backstage, who in turn signaled to me. Somehow, there was a communication snafu and the wrong signals led to the wrong girl winning the date. However, after I had dinner with the winner, I went out with the other girl anyway.

After the contest, I went to see Kelly for a week because I found out she had broken up with her boyfriend. I wanted to have sex with her and I tried my damnedest. But Kelly knew about Paula, and I think Kelly always felt her in the room with us and flat-out refused my advances.

"No. You have a girlfriend."

She was adamant, and although I knew sex wasn't going to happen, I did convince her to help me out in other ways in that department. I didn't tell Paula about this when I came home, but I'm sure she knew something had transpired.

After my big win, I thought my life would dramatically change, and when someone at NBC asked me for a meeting, I showed up with high hopes, which were dashed when the project went nowhere. I couldn't seem to get my life going again, I couldn't get traction.

One day not long after winning the contest, I looked at my bottle of lithium pills and then studied my reflection. I was only twenty-three. Did I really need these meds? I had won a major contest, and I was feeling fine except for how I felt on these pills. It took away the edge and I thought I needed that edge, thought that the creative highs and lows and dramatic emotions were tools for my profession. That young macho part of me felt I didn't need a crutch and blamed the lithium for everything I hadn't yet achieved. It convinced me I could do it by myself. And so I put the pill bottle down without opening it. The next day I still felt good, and so I did the same thing. And the next day. And the next.

Soon, the days turned into a few months.

Meanwhile, things were as normal in the house as they could be given our unusual arrangement, and Paula continued to accompany me to parties and events when I asked her, often with my parents. One night we all went to a Bar Mitzvah and the entire night girls were coming up to me and flirting, right in front of Paula, which frustrated her because I didn't stop them and didn't make her feel any better about it.

After the party, we all got in the car and the lid blew when I asked Paula, "What's wrong with you?"

"That wasn't very nice, flirting with all those girls," she answered.

My father did what he wanted in his marriage, and had his own opinion on the matter and let her know it. "So what if they love him, Paula, you have to respect Mauricio. You have to respect him or you're going to be crying tears of blood!" he declared with his thick accent and usual flair.

Paula and I laugh about that now, but that night it wasn't funny. While my mom watched my father rip into Paula, she said nothing, but then again, neither did I, because that's what I had learned, that was the macho way. Paula bawled all the way home that night, but she needed to survive—and living at our house was surviving—so she learned how to do just that. It must have been very painful for her to fall deeper in love with me and not immediately get that love back, but somewhere inside she knew that this was right. Wise beyond her years because she had been through so much at such a young age, Paula knew we were supposed to be together, she knew that the real attraction was a deeper bond, born out of dark times in both our lives. Paula's philosophy was firm and simple: if you love something, set if free, and if it comes back to you, it's yours forever, and if it doesn't, it was never yours to begin with. So, although she was vulnerable, Paula lived with me and put up with me and gave me space to find my way back to her.

Years later in Los Angeles, a therapist, one of the many who have guided me over the years in my search for self-enlightenment, helped me recognize what a caveman I could be. I am grateful that I came to see I needed to be a better man, partner, and husband, but before I got to that point of understanding, I put Paula through a lot.

Despite everything, I was a lucky man. I just didn't realize how lucky at the time.

CHAPTER SIX

God Part II

During that time I was determined to get my career right, so I pressed on and before long started getting roles in plays. I *loved* being onstage in front of an audience because the applause I craved as a little boy singing "Ben" was now multiplied tenfold and heady. When I garnered some good reviews onstage in San Francisco in *Three Views of Mount Fuji* and *Community at Risk*, I felt like I was on my way. I was in a metropolitan city that was not only exploding with theater and culture, but in the eighties San Francisco was the home of many bands, and a new upstart TV station, MTV, was playing music videos twenty-four hours a day, reinvigorating the dying music industry. A plethora of music videos were shooting constantly, so I decided to try out for one that the band R.O.A.R., comprised of members from Carlos Santana's band, was casting, but they wanted someone who was Italian and the name Mauricio Jose Morales didn't exactly scream Italian.

I didn't get a callback, so I decided in order to work and get preconceptions out of the heads of those making the casting decisions, I would change my name. Once again, Michael Olten pressured me to use the name Rick Madrid, but instead I took my grandmother's maiden name—Benard—and shortened my first name to Maurice, and that is how Mauricio Jose Morales became Maurice Benard. It's ironic: for years most people thought I was Italian because of my new name and because I played Sonny as an Italian, even though I found out a month or so after I started at *General Hospital* playing him that way that he was Cuban and Greek.

I may have changed my name, but I'm still proud of my heritage—it's good to have brown skin and it's nice to see so much of it on-screen now, although there's always room for more. One of my favorite movies is *El Cantante*, an amazing film with Jennifer Lopez and Marc Anthony. There was a time when that movie probably wouldn't have gotten made, but now media is far more diverse, which is important. I can still remember the time, because it wasn't long ago, when basically everyone on TV was white.

Yet another person to join the team of Maurice Benard at that time was Alan Drew, a short, heavyset older man who became not only my teacher but my mentor. He was very intuitive and even predicted my success as an actor long before I truly believed it was possible. I knew from watching videos of my performances that, while I wasn't good, I could *become* good with time and a lot of hard work, which I was more than willing to do. I had never cared about anything this much in my life, including cars or the many different girls in my world, and was convinced if I worked at it, I could be the next Al Pacino.

And then, out of the blue, I got a call from Jimmy that R.O.A.R. was giving me the job in the video after all, because

Carlos Santana had contacted legendary San Francisco promoter Bill Graham, who called R.O.A.R. Someone at the audition had seen something in me, I guess, even though it was raw, regardless of my last name and my brown skin, and lobbied for me, and to this day I wish I knew who it was so I could say thank you.

The video was my first paid acting job and it felt incredible. My character was a fighter, a big brother, and a bad boy who realizes he has to change his ways to be a role model for his younger brother, which I thought was ironic, given that I was the bad boy in my family. We shot for two days in a moody, cool setting in a big warehouse in San Francisco and I loved every minute of it. It felt familiar, like the little boy singing "Ben" to a room full of spectators, or dancing at the clubs and in the competitions in high school, with everyone watching and clapping. Silently prancing for the fashion world was one thing, but performing in front of a camera, to music, was an entirely different sensation—it was creative and fun and I wanted to do more. Things truly seemed to be headed in the right direction and I chased that road more than ever.

But had the pressure to be somebody and the nonstop obsession with acting taken a toll?

One night, a few months after I had stopped taking my lithium, Paula and I went to the mall to hang out, as we often did, and I was hell-bent on buying her anything she wanted. As we walked through the stores browsing, I was suddenly drawn to a lacquered wood painting of Jesus and insisted on purchasing it for her. We took it home and hung it in our room at my parents' house. Shortly after that, when Paula was at work one night, I was reading and when I looked up, the Jesus on the wall had morphed into the devil. I quickly turned the lights off so the terrifying demon wouldn't look back at me. I was shaking with fright, my heartbeat rapidly pounding in my ears.

God, I'm not ready for this, I'm not ready to die, I prayed, certain the devil was coming for me.

Suddenly the devil picture hurtled off the shelf of its own accord and fell crashing to the floor, and I jumped, afraid of what might happen next. Still trembling, I stared at the wooden Jesus face down on the floor, afraid to touch it, but after a few moments reached for it, and as I turned it over slowly, a beautiful warm gold light flooded the room and the devil face disappeared. Instead, Jesus gazed back at me compassionately and, although the painting had flown off the shelf from a good height, it was still in pristine condition, without a dent, scratch, or scuff on it. It was as if an unseen hand had exorcised the devil from the painting, and I believed the devil had been there with the same conviction I believed that God had come to save me.

A few days later I had an interview with the local morning show on ABC, *AM San Francisco*, as America's Most Watchable Man, and when they presented me with a gift someone had sent in care of the station, I opened the box to find a beautiful cross from Jerusalem. I couldn't take my eyes off it and suddenly had an intense urge to find a church where I could take confession, so I abruptly left the station and began walking, asking random strangers where I could find the closest cathedral. The more I walked, the deeper the sense of urgency grew to talk to a priest.

Then I began running, as if the devil inside me had to get out, and when I saw a church, I barreled toward it, but it was locked. I ran to the next one only to find the doors were bolted as well, so I ran farther and was encouraged to finally see a light on in a mission, where I knocked relentlessly until a man answered the door.

I was told everyone had gone to bed but I pleaded to see the father and handed the cross to the man, begging him to take it inside and tell the Father I needed to confess.

He disappeared back inside and I waited awhile, and just when I was turning to go, the monsignor appeared and led me inside and down a corridor to the chapel. The cross had persuaded the monsignor, and he asked what was troubling me.

"I saw God in my room," I told him, relating the events that had happened.

The monsignor listened, and when I was finished he put his hand over mine, placing the cross in my hand. "I don't know if you saw the devil or God . . . I can't tell you what it was, but don't be afraid."

I suddenly felt a sense of peace, and after I finished talking with the Father I returned to the street only to realize I had run so far, I had to call a taxi to get back home that night.

I hand't had a full-blown breakdown like when my parents admitted me to the mental institution, but the manic episode had unnerved me, as well as Paula and my parents, and I thought it was probably better to start taking my lithium again.

Once I did, the religious visions calmed down and it looked like my life was finally going to turn around. It started with a call in 1987 from my agency at the time, Stars, who put me on videotape and submitted the tape to ABC to consider me for several new roles on the network's popular soap opera *All My Children*. I was stunned and excited, and my first thought was how much my dad loved the show and how often we had argued about my future while it was on TV in his living room. I remembered yelling at him that it was the only job that would make him proud of me, and smiled at the irony.

73

After watching my performance, the executives liked what they saw and flew me to New York to audition in person for the producers. I had never been to New York and I was traveling alone. The city seemed very big, so I have to admit I was scared and just getting through the flight took everything inside me. Once I got to the hotel room, I had that familiar antsy feeling and needed to run, so I sprinted to Central Park and kept running until I almost dropped, listening to "Eye of the Tiger" over and over on my portable CD player.

The next day, sitting in the audition room with a bunch of other guys who looked just like me didn't help my nerves much, but I got through the reading and thought I was good. I waited with all the other guys for the outcome, staring at the producer when he came out, on pins and needles to hear whose life was going to change.

"We found our guy," the producer announced to the room.

But it wasn't me. My heart sank and I went back to my hotel room to prepare for the flight back to San Francisco in the morning, but after a few hours the phone rang.

"Can you come in and audition for another role?" the voice on the other end asked.

My spirits soared—they liked me! So the next day I auditioned again, and again I waited for what seemed like forever for a producer to come back out with a verdict.

"We found our guy. Thanks everyone, best of luck," he said, shaking another actor's hand and ushering him back behind closed doors.

I was crushed and stared at the closed door for a long while before returning to my hotel room for the second disappointing night, where I immediately threw all my things into my luggage, more than ready to get the hell out of New York. I was interrupted by the phone and I picked up thinking it was Paula, bracing myself to tell her the bad news, however it wasn't Paula on the other end.

"You didn't get either of the roles . . . but we're creating a role just for you," the producer said. I wasn't sure I had heard him right, but he continued, "You did a fabulous job, congratulations."

The role they created was a character that would become wildly popular almost instantly—I would be playing Nico Kelly, a young rough type, the nephew of bad guy Creed. I had gotten a job on an actual TV show and it wasn't just a one-off job, it was a *contract* role. I hung up and let it sink in for just a moment, then dialed Paula because I couldn't wait to tell her the good news. It was so good to hear her voice on the phone when she picked up.

"Hi, babe, you okay?" she asked.

"Yeah, actually, I'm great."

"The audition went okay?" she asked. "Do you have to stay and do more?"

"I think the third time was the charm," I joked.

"They liked you?" she pressed.

"They not only liked me, they created a role for me, babe, a contract role!"

I heard a little yelp of joy on the other end. "Honey, that's so great! I knew you could do it!" she said, and then she was silent a moment before broaching the obvious subject. "So I guess that means living in New York." She was wondering what me living in New York meant for her, but I hadn't gotten to that thought yet in my mind.

"Yeah, New York." There was another awkward pause before I ended the call. "Well, look, I wanted to tell you and now I'm gonna pack and see if I can get an earlier flight out."

"Okay, I love you," she said.

Although it didn't come easily to me, I said I loved her, too. Once I was on the plane back to San Francisco, I had hours to think about everything that had happened and what it meant for my future. I kept hearing Paula's voice, the absolute certainty in it, and I kept seeing her face, smiling at me, always encouraging me. I think that was the moment I realized nothing ever seemed real until I told her about it and that we were in this thing together.

I may have said a thousand times I was going to move to Los Angeles with my buddies, but now that my future was calling, I couldn't imagine moving anywhere without Paula and I couldn't wait to get home to tell her—and ask if she would join me. When I got off the plane, Paula was standing in the baggage claim to pick me up. She hugged me tight and kissed me and I held on to her for dear life, then she looked into my face, sensing something was different.

"Honey, what is it? What's going on?"

I looked at her and kissed her again. "I want you to move to New York with me," I said.

And at that, Paula threw her arms around me and kissed me deeply.

"I take that as a yes," I teased.

It was what Paula was hoping for, but given our history, and my inability to commit, something she wasn't sure would or could happen yet.

"I'd go to the moon and back," she whispered in my ear, kissing me again.

Because *All My Children* wanted me to start immediately, we barely had time to say goodbye to everyone, so my parents threw a party at the house and Manny and Jeff and all my friends were so excited we stayed up all night talking. Paula and I left for the airport the next day with only a few small suitcases—and lots of big dreams. A guy I knew had moved to New York earlier, and when he found out we were moving to the city, he found a place and rented it for us, so we moved into the small apartment in Hell's Kitchen on Fifty-Third and Ninth sight unseen. It was right next to an animal shelter, so we both took that as a sign it was where we were supposed to be.

My first day at work was Paula's nineteenth birthday and she walked me to the ABC studio on Sixty-Sixth and Columbus, a routine that continued the entire time we lived there. It was the first day of the rest of my career and I was nervous, and meeting Michael Knight and Susan Lucci that day exacerbated the feeling. It was intimidating because I had watched them on the show when I was a teenager and never thought one day it would be my destiny to work with them. I was so driven I wanted to learn as much as I possibly could in the two years of my contract before I headed back out West to L.A., only not with Manny and Jeff like we had talked about, it would be with Paula, and nothing would stand in the way of my success as an actor.

The *All My Children* producers had no idea I suffered from bipolar disorder, because an acting coach had told me not to tell people about it or I would never get hired. I sure as hell wasn't going to screw up my big chance, so I hid it and I hid it well.

The pressure was now on, and on a whole new terrifying scale. The need to prove myself, just as it had been throughout my childhood, was immense, and although I didn't have much dialogue and was only in a few scenes that first day, I was determined to stand out. When the fan mail started pouring in after I had been there a few weeks I finally lost that sense of being on the outside looking in.

Nico and Tad Martin shared story lines and I enjoyed doing scenes with Michael Knight. Off set we had fun, too, because he's got a great sense of humor. I also became friends with Cameron Mathison, who's a great guy.

But I worked long hours and was pushing myself to the limit on *All My Children*. I was taking my meds, so I thought things would stay calm, but I had stopped therapy when I left Dr. Noonan and San Francisco without finding a new doctor in New York, ignoring the possibility that it would cost me down the line. Being bipolar doesn't just go away one day; it's something you have to manage every day, your whole life. I had barely begun to understand my condition and had not mastered all the tools to control *it* instead of letting it control *me*.

Since I was gone from early in the morning until late at night, Paula wanted an animal to keep her company, but since my parents had always told me I was allergic after one ill-fated dog rescue, I believed that and told Paula. Even though we had a tiny apartment, Paula really wanted a dog, and after researching decided a toy poodle would affect my allergies the least, so we got one in the city and named him Nyco after my character on *All My Children*. I had zero allergic reaction to him, so a few months after that, I came home from an event with a beautiful charcoal-gray kitten I also clearly wasn't allergic to. I named him Charlie, after one of my character's rivals.

When I wasn't working, Paula and I hung out with the friend who had found the apartment for us, but after a while it became clear he was schizophrenic when he started talking in different voices and exhibited other bizarre behavior. It went downhill quickly from there when he became extremely possessive and that turned into stalking, calling constantly from morning to night, and even calling my dad to insist I was gay and Paula was my cover. My father told him off but he threatened to "tell the world" about me, and no matter what we tried, he refused to get any help. His increasing outbursts really shook us, so we wondered if he would start getting violent, and, unable to help him, we finally took ourselves out of the situation and moved to a nice neighborhood in Jersey City to share a two-bedroom flat with Michael Hawthorne, a model we had met who became and still is a dear friend. Our landlord lived below us and didn't mind the animals—or that we would add more when a tiny Pomeranian we named Mitzy joined the brood.

While I was working, Paula temped doing secretarial work before getting a job at the World Trade Center preschool, which she enjoyed because she loved being around children and hoped more than anything to have her own someday. She still wasn't in contact with her mother, but not long after we moved to Jersey City, Paula's brother, John, also came to stay with us. John was a wild, troubled teen who would disappear for days—and even though Paula had no idea knew where he was, she didn't get angry and was always patient with him. Paula still had a sort of survivor's guilt for escaping her childhood situation while her brother and sister had stayed and endured physical abuse, so Paula has spent the rest of her life making it up to him.

While Paula was taking care of John, I started getting mobbed on the streets making my way to and from work, because in those days, when I got there before our seven a.m. start time, fans were already gathered outside the studio, waiting for the actors to show up. I had to wade through a sea of people shouting my name and requesting photos and autographs, and when we finished at seven p.m. I faced another group of fans who wanted the same thing. Although at first it seemed odd for total strangers to act like they knew me, I realized they were why I was working and I always stopped and tried to talk to everybody and sign headshots.

One of my most memorable encounters with a fan was when a friend from acting class wanted me to come to lunch one day to meet none other than Luther Vandross, who, as it turns out, was a huge *All My Children* and Nico fan, and I thought it was wild that my hero had become my fan. I walked into the restaurant and he flashed that giant magic smile like he'd known me forever, thrilled to hear that I had seen him sing in San Francisco before he was famous and knew he'd hit it big, and for years, whenever I was in New York, it was always fun to run into him.

Shortly after I started on the show, fans nominated me for the *Soap Opera Digest* Outstanding Male Newcomer Award and the same loyal *Soap Opera Digest* fans would go on to nominate me multiple times over the years for various categories, including Hottest Soap Couple, shared with Vanessa Marcil; Favorite Couple, shared with Sarah Brown; and they would bestow to me the Outstanding Lead Actor Award twice and Favorite Actor Award as well. Since Nico was so popular, the producers began adding more story lines for my character.

More story lines meant more girls, so I had a lot of screen tests making out with young actresses, which upset Paula, and the jealousy that had always been a danger zone in our relationship kicked into high gear. Looking back, I don't blame Paula, because of my past behavior; of course she felt insecure with all the actresses because of all the actresses from class I had gone out with while she was living with me in Martinez. I didn't help the situation when women were throwing themselves at me on the street or when I traveled alone for press or when someone asked if I was married and I answered no, failing to clarify that I was living with someone in a relationship that had been going on for years. Again, that is on me. I still had that macho wiring and was clueless. I thought because we weren't married yet, I still had some wild oats to sow, and I felt Paula should understand that.

During that time, Paula read every script and counted every scene I was slated to perform with a female actress. It got so bad she even counted the number of kisses, and we argued over that constantly. I had a hard time understanding her insecurity, partly because I couldn't come to terms with my role in it. The other part, which was important, was that the whole time I truly believed she was my angel. After all, Paula is gorgeous inside and out, the most amazing woman I know. She has a huge heart and the smarts to match, but back then she didn't see how I see her, and sometimes even now doesn't realize when total strangers think she's a knock-out. Whenever we went to parties, men were always flirting with her. One of them was Jack Nicholson, who couldn't stop staring at her when we met at an event at Paramount.

One image that is forever seared into my brain is from a vacation in Puerto Rico while we were at the El Conquistador's private beach. Paula was swimming in the ocean and when she emerged, with wet hair and shimmering drops of water cascading down her body and over the red two-piece bikini she was wearing, I swear it was like the waters parting and the Bond Girl appearing. I could hardly breathe. I was filming her with one of those bulky video cameras in vogue at the time and as she moved toward me and the camera, skin glistening, lips forming a smile, I realized all the people on the beach had stopped to stare at her. But her mother did a real number on her self-image, and when I showed Paula the footage, she hated it and never wore a two-piece bathing suit again.

It would take a while for Paula to become confident and for me to give her more of a reason to feel that way, but before that, the jealousy kept rearing its head and we argued time and again.

Soon after that first year in New York I felt cornered in my life. I knew I needed room to breathe and decided to go back home to Martinez without Paula to get some space. While I was there of course I hung out with Jeff and Manny, and one night we went to a club in the city. Although Jeff got drunk, as usual, he insisted on driving us home, so Manny sat in the front and I got in the backseat and Jeff rolled down all the windows. It was ten degrees outside and I was freezing and kept asking him to roll the windows up, but Jeff just laughed as the wind whipped through the car and my teeth chattered. During the forty-five-minute drive to my parents' house, no matter how much I begged Jeff he wouldn't roll up the windows, and when we finally got to my parents' place I was furious, maybe a little manic, too, so when I stepped out of the car, I exploded.

"Fuck you, Jeff!" I screamed.

"Fuck you, Maurice!" he retorted.

"We're done!" I said, and just like that we stopped talking, and as time went by, I think we were both too proud, or stubborn, or stupid to apologize and step up and repair the relationship.

Although the argument with Jeff put a damper on the trip, Manny had a date and told me she had a friend, so we agreed that when he brought them over, if I mentioned that the "concert" was great, I would go out with them. If not, I'd pass. When Manny and his date showed up, the gorgeous girl with them walked in and smiled and I immediately looked at Manny and told him the "concert" was *amazing*. We all went to the club, and one thing, of course, led to another, I took the girl home, and I was convinced I was into her when I left for New York.

I didn't tell Paula about her, but I continued to talk to her on the phone and did plan to see her when she came to visit me in New York. What I did tell Paula was that I needed two days alone and I was going to stay in my dressing room at *All My Children*, which led to a huge argument. When the girl showed up, we went out on the town, but it quickly became a total nightmare and whatever I thought I had wanted from her on my break in San Francisco wasn't working at all back in my real world. I managed to get out of seeing her the rest of her stay in the city and later found out she wasted no time and hooked up with one of my actor friends from *All My Children*, but I guess I deserved that as well as the fallout with Paula that followed my stag weekend.

Paula didn't know about the girl, but she knew something was wrong and I wasn't treating her well, and she was right. At the time, I had no excuse, because I wasn't having a breakdown and I was on my meds—I was just behaving like a selfish, macho guy. Paula truly thought it was over between us once and for all, so she followed the philosophy she had always clung to and left me a voice mail telling me she was willing to set me free because she loved me. That set-it-free quote seemed dumb to me at the time. If you love something set it free and if it is yours it will come back to you—I had no idea what that even meant.

That night I had a terrible dream and in it I was accepting an Academy Award and thanking Paula, but she couldn't hear me because she was in a coffin, which scared me and startled me awake.

I was so bereft and shaken at the thought of Paula being gone forever I had to make up for everything and get her back, so I bought a beautiful pair of really expensive earrings as a token of my remorse and took them to her at the apartment. I admitted to her I was an idiot and didn't want to lose her, relating the dream and how much it upset me, and hoped I hadn't screwed our relationship up for good. Paula listened and knew I was sincere, so she accepted my gift and apology, now having even more faith in her philosophy than ever before because she had set me free and I had returned.

After I resolved things with Paula, life was finally good, and she wasn't my only cheerleader anymore, because now that I was on TV, my parents thought I had chosen the perfect profession, and although they already watched *All My Children* every single day, now they tuned in with pride. I had proven to them, to my brother, to Jimmy, and to everyone from my hometown that I could be a star, but a restlessness gnawed at me and I wasn't content with the soap opera my father was so pleased employed me. It wasn't enough. Something was driving me, more than my need to succeed, more than my competitive streak from childhood, more than my fear that I couldn't make it in movies if I stayed in New York. That same ethereal manic anxiety that pushed me to go running like a devil, past exhaustion, was chasing me again.

So I ran, this time from my contract, and told the producers I had decided to leave *All My Children* when it expired. They were shocked, and because they didn't want to kill Nico, they asked me to extend my stay an extra three months so they could craft an exit story, leaving an open door for me to return at any time. I agreed to be there long enough to do the character justice, so after going on the run with Tad and Dixie, played by the wonderful Cady

McClain, my character and Cecily, portrayed by Rosa Nevin, who had hated each other, fell in love, and Nico proposed. After their romantic wedding in Hawaii they decided not to return to Pine Valley and I was free to leave New York. In real life, Cady went on to marry Jon Lindstrom, who has kicked ass as Dr. Kevin Collins on *General Hospital*, and been a good friend, for years.

Although the fans were sad when I left the show, I felt like it was a new beginning—for my career, for my life, and for my relationship with Paula. She had been there for me and through everything with me and I finally *got* it—I knew that I didn't need to search for love anymore because it was right in front of me. I didn't need to sow my oats anymore because I was ready to commit to the one person who understood me, the one person who had always believed in me, and loved me unconditionally, no matter how dark my life had gotten at times, and no matter how much I'd screwed up.

I never fell in love with the city like so many people do, so it wasn't hard to say goodbye to my life there when we packed up our apartment in Jersey City and left the East Coast. Once we were back in Martinez, my parents and I threw a party for Paula's twenty-first birthday in a venue near San Francisco where a fellow actor friend, Angelo Pagán, now married to Leah Remini, was our musical entertainment for the evening. As he finished a song and the band finished playing, I took the microphone and, just as I had when I was a kid, pulled the crowd in, this time with a passionate speech about Paula, my beautiful angel, who meant everything to me. Not one to like attention, Paula was embarrassed at first, but when I finished my soliloquy by presenting an engagement ring to her in front of family and friends, she forgot about being shy. After all the time she had stood by me through my manic episodes, all she had gone through being secondary to my career, and waiting for me when it was difficult to wait . . . after always living with the uncertainty that I might find distraction or love in another woman, Paula was overjoyed for me to finally commit to her and ask her to commit to me.

It was like a switch flipped inside me the day I asked her to marry me. I never wanted another woman again and I never cheated like the macho generations in my family.

Paula likes to correct my version of the story and remembers it the same way except for one small detail—Paula says I never actually popped the question, I just *announced* that we were getting married. That's the beauty of our relationship—it works in so many ways when it's not supposed to.

CHAPTER SEVEN

Welcome to the Jungle

Our adventure in New York was over, and in 1990 Paula and I were back on the West Coast, but this time we were living in the mecca of movies: Hollywood. We rented a house in West Los Angeles with a yard for the dogs. While I auditioned for films, Paula planned the storybook wedding she had always wanted. Hollywood was a mecca to me because it was the center of the film universe, but for Paula it was special for another reason: Disneyland. For the girl who had a dark and violent childhood, who had seen too many things too soon, it was where she could finally claim that childhood joy and bliss. For her it really was the happiest place on earth.

So it is not surprising that the theme for our nuptials was inspired by the Magic Kingdom and featured a puffy Cinderella gown and glass slippers. My mom helped Paula plan the big event, including handcrafting tiny pillows with glass slippers sewn to them as party favors for the special occasion, but in the midst of all the planning, I was cast in a TV movie, so the storybook wedding, much like our very first date, was not meant to be—not for a while anyway.

We canceled the huge celebration, Paula preserved the dress in a box in the closet, and on August 11, 1990, Paula and I exchanged vows in my parents' backyard in Martinez. Paula didn't want to jinx the full-on dream wedding she knew would happen *someday*, so instead of white she wore a sexy black minidress and I wore a suit. We did, however, include two traditions that were very sentimental for us, involving my father as well as her nieces.

Paula hadn't spoken to her mother since she had left home, but she did talk to her sister, Stephanie, who still lived in the flophouse and now had another child, Angie. Paula drove to get Angie and her other niece, Vanessa, and brought them back, clothing them in cute little dresses and as I stood there in the garden watching them scatter petals as my father walked Paula "down the aisle" toward me, I knew it was a moment I would always remember, the moment my life really started.

Paula wanted to save the rest of the special wedding details—including the Cinderella dress and photos memorializing the day—for a later date. None of Paula's other relatives were at the wedding, but Manny and the rest of our friends were there to toast us with my family. Although it wasn't the wedding Paula had dreamed about since she was little, she was happy about this new beginning—we were finally married.

After we said our vows I started shooting *Her Wicked Ways* in the role of Steve, and once I finished that, I started auditioning for numerous shows. Paula wanted to have children and I did, too, someday, but for now I was focused on other things, mostly my career. I have to admit, deep down I was also afraid of having kids and what that would do to our relationship. So we talked about it and decided to wait. Paula soon found a way to scratch that strong maternal itch by getting involved with HOLA (Heart of Los Angeles), an amazing organization that gives underserved kids an equal chance to succeed through after-school academics, arts, athletics, and wellness programs. Every weekend we mentored teens, playing football or basketball, depending on the time of year. Paula was right there on the field, literally down in the dirt, and that's another thing I adore about her. She *loves* sports, whether it's watching, playing, or talking about them. She's more passionate about sports than anyone I know, and not only is that fun but it's incredibly sexy.

We already had a lot of animals to shower attention on, but one day, about six months after moving to Los Angeles, I was shopping at Century City Mall, the sprawling outdoor venue between Beverly Hills and Santa Monica I loved because it had—and still has—so many cool stores and restaurants and a multiplex theater where you could spend the whole day. Back then there were still pet stores in malls, and I could never walk past one without going in to see what kind of animals were there or pick several up to play with them.

This particular day, I was killing time before going to a movie and went into the pet store like I always did, and the first thing I saw were English bulldog puppies who were vocal and squirming around seeking attention. As I walked over, I locked eyes with the biggest, ugliest, cutest one in the pack, and as I looked at him and he looked at me there was an instant connection. I couldn't walk out of that store without him, so I brought the puppy home and named him Corleone, after the character Michael Corleone in *The Godfather*. Corleone was wild as a puppy and happy all the time. It definitely wouldn't be the last time I surprised Paula with another pet.

I had signed with APA in New York for representation but when I moved to L.A., I signed with Triad. I continued to audition and finally did a guest role on the ABC sitcom *Stat*. But things were tight, so in order to save money, we downsized and moved across the street from the house we were occupying to an apartment. And then a role came up that initially I did not want to do, a TV movie about the life of Desi Arnaz and Lucille Ball: *Lucy & Desi: Before the Laughter*. I learned about it from my agent at Triad, when he floated the idea of me auditioning for the role of Desi during dinner with me and my dad, who happened to be in town visiting.

"Forget it," I said bluntly.

My dad, never one to hold his tongue, chimed in, "He'd be perfect!"

It took the entire dinner, but my father and my agent worked on me until they finally talked me into agreeing to audition. I wasn't too nervous because I didn't care about the part, and the audition went well, or so I thought. It would have been fine if they told me I didn't get it, which was a first for me, to feel unencumbered by nerves and pressure. After months went by with no word, I figured that was that; I had lost the part.

However, one day my agent called with news that the producers wanted me back for another audition, so I went back in. Only this time the nerves kicked in and I knew it didn't go well. I had no doubt I would lose the part. Had I messed up on purpose? Or did I really want the part now and psyched myself out? The more I second-guessed myself, the harder it was to wait for the outcome, and I was surprised when, after several more months, my agent told me the producers wanted to see me again.

This time I made sure I studied and watched old footage, trying to get the Desi voice. I still wasn't sure I wanted the role, but I was sure I wanted to prove to them that I could do it. While I was waiting to audition, Michael St. Gerard, an actor I knew who had played Elvis in a miniseries, was sitting next to me and, as we chatted, I voiced my reservations. Michael told me not to resist the role and not to overthink it.

"Just do it," was his parting advice.

When I got into the room for the third audition, the producers were austere and intimidating, looking me up and down critically.

"What makes you think you can play Desi?" one of the people at the table asked.

I didn't hesitate. "Because my father is just like Desi." And that was the truth, because as a kid I had watched him at parties, larger than life, always flirting and entertaining.

The producers eyed me, unsure, and after a long beat they asked me to go in the bathroom, slick my hair back, and then return to read. So I did, yet the producers were still wavering and wanted more. Next, I had to do a screen test with Frances Fisher, who was playing Lucy. I had never done a screen test before and was already nervous when I got to the soundstage and I became even more nervous when the executive producer, Larry Thompson, with his signature ponytail, stood right by the camera, watching. I knew it was cocky, but I asked if they could get him to leave and Thompson disappeared. I figured I had probably pissed him off, but at least I had given the screen test my best shot, so I was surprised when they called to tell me I finally got the role and was equally surprised I was happy about it.

The first morning I was due on set, I was feeling great. When I reached for my pill bottle, I hesitated. It had been so long since my breakdown, I had been out of the hospital for three years and the last time I went off lithium, years ago, I didn't have a violent breakdown. I didn't realize—or maybe hadn't accepted yet—that mine was a lifelong condition and would require lifelong medication. Once again, that macho voice inside me figured I could handle it; my head told me I didn't need meds because I wasn't sick, and I put the pill bottle back in the medicine cabinet.

Paula was thrilled about the movie and we decided to splurge and rent a house in the Hollywood Hills with a beautiful view. While I was at work, Paula settled us and the animals into our new digs.

There was one small problem—I had Desi down, but I just couldn't get the singing no matter how hard I tried. It stressed me out and worried me, but when I voiced my doubt to the director, Charles Jarrett, he didn't flinch.

"This is the deal, Maurice—we have eighteen days to shoot this and five thousand yards of film," he told me.

So I didn't give up and we kept doing take after take, and finally I got through the musical demands of the film. Although the singing had been hard, I loved doing scenes with Frances Fischer, because not only is she an amazing actress, she's a wonderful person, and we had fun during the shoot. At the time, she was with Clint Eastwood, and my one regret during filming is that I was asleep in my trailer when he came to the set and I didn't meet him, though he's another one of those icons in my book.

When we wrapped, I couldn't wait to show the film to my friends because I thought, *No doubt, I'm Al Pacino now*, however, I didn't get quite the reaction from my friends I anticipated and, in fact, most of them hated it. They weren't alone—the critics were ruthless, and although I was devastated, I still wanted to read every single brutal review. They called me things like Speedy Gonzales on cocaine, and on top of that, Johnny Carson even came out on his show and told his viewing audience to boycott the TV movie in deference to the family. I still remember every harsh word, every mean comment, all these years later, but regardless of the critics, the film got decent ratings and in true Hollywood style I even received flowers from the president of the network, Jeff Sagansky.

A month later, however, I was broke again, and standing in the unemployment line with people staring at me and finally mustering the nerve to ask, "Weren't you Nico on *All My Children*? Weren't you Desi?"

It was humiliating.

Although I had gotten small roles in some independent films that were a creative outlet for me, including Diego in *Ruby* and Creeper in *Mi Vida Loca*, I didn't get paid enough money to cover the bills. Another example of classic Hollywood that caused problems for me was shooting a film but never knowing when it would be released or if I would end up in the final cut, and, to my dismay, my character was cut from *Mi Vida Loca*. The only way you get your next gig is because people saw your last gig on TV or in the theater, so it was like I'd never done the film, and that didn't help at all. Once again, we couldn't afford the steep rent, and begged the landlord to let us break the lease and move out—luckily, he agreed. When we found an affordable house to rent in Studio City, we thought things would get easier; however, six months later our former landlord took us to court and sued us for the rest of the money. It seemed like no matter how hard I tried, things just kept getting worse.

Meanwhile, Paula began doing extra work on many films and TV shows to bring in money and in hopes of meeting someone who would give me a break in a movie. She managed to get a two-week job as an extra, a member of the jury, in the film *Body of Evidence*, starring Madonna, Willem Dafoe, and Joe Mantegna. At lunch, Dafoe and Mantegna graciously listened to her talk about her actor husband, and the veteran actors even had me come to the set one day to meet them.

Another time, she was asked to test as the body double for Winona Ryder in *Dracula*, and even though it required shooting topless, she thought if it would help me, she'd do it, imagining my delight at being on set with Francis Ford Coppola. Paula was petrified and nervous through the whole two days she was on hold, but as it turned out, she was very tan at the time and Ryder was not, so she was released, and, frankly, relieved.

Paula also began waitressing to cover the bills, and I immersed myself with studying the craft of acting, enrolling in the Howard Fine Acting Studio. My first impression of the six-foot-tall, dark-haired teacher was that Howard seemed wise beyond his years, truly a savant, very serious, and extremely kind. One day, during a scene from *Zoo Story*, when I began crying Howard stopped the scene.

"You need to see me after class," he said.

He continued with class, and when it ended I lingered behind as the other students trickled out. When they were gone, he closed the door and gave it to me straight.

"That's the worst acting I've ever seen," he told me. The words cut me to the core, but he continued, "Your talent is there, but your technique is horrible. Because I believe in you, and I understand that you don't have a spare dime, I'm going to teach you for free. You can pay me back later."

I appreciated his honesty and his offer to help, so I bought a tape recorder and took it with me every week to work with him, and after months of one-on-one training I did a monologue from *Danny and the Deep Blue Sea*, playing a character who wants to kill himself. I had grown a beard and walked in completely in character, and when I finished my monologue Howard looked at me a beat and shook his head proudly.

"You're Danny. You're done," he said.

He was an amazing teacher because he showed me how to really *become* a character and *feel* an emotion instead of playing one. Howard was impressed with my progress, but he was worried that there was danger in a fragile emotional person going so deep into method preparation. He suggested I audition for sitcoms and balance out the heavy drama. I still had no luck; even when I auditioned for the Actors Studio, I wasn't asked to join. I was disappointed again and again. It was a constant struggle for two long years, so it's no wonder the intense pressure began to take its toll.

Not only was my ego crushed, I was ashamed that my new wife worked all day, every day, to pay the bills. When we couldn't make ends meet my parents also had to help financially. The more the pressure mounted, the worse I felt, and, angry, frustrated, and depressed, I began making some bad decisions, like going to strip clubs with my new buddies Ray and Danny.

Danny, who had dated a former costar of mine on *All My Children*, had the same weird sense of humor as me, and we shared a passion for acting. Ray and I had become friends while attending the same acting class in Malibu and also talked about acting and movies all the time. He was a cowboy who did the best impersonation of Elvis I had ever seen or heard. Since Paula is an avid Elvis fan, I always had him call her as Elvis and sing, which Paula loved.

Although I had borrowed money from Ray, I didn't have to spend any at the club because they knew me as Nico from *All My Children* and were fans, so I always got free drinks. The dancers knew me as well, so they danced for me and Ray and Danny without expecting big tips. But despite the good time I had hanging out with the guys, I felt bad that Paula was working and I wasn't. I felt inadequate, I was drinking, and at this point I had been off of lithium and therapy for two years without thinking about what a disastrous combination that was.

At the club I always talked to one dancer in particular and

even convinced myself I had fallen for her. One night I walked her to her car and leaned in to kiss her and she pulled away, looking into my very soul, like Kelly had years ago.

"Go home to your wife," she said. I knew I'd never try that again. I also knew she was right and I had almost made a terrible mistake. I couldn't wait to get home to see Paula, but when I walked into the house, I knew something else was wrong.

I finally got it out of Paula that she had heard from her sister that her mother had adopted a three-week-old baby girl named Heather—the second child she had adopted in two years. Both children were born to Paula's cousin, and both were taken by the state before Paula's mom filed to adopt them. Paula was deeply worried about another child having to live in the same conditions she had grown up in. She felt helpless that there was nothing she could do, but she still had no relationship with her mother. For once, it was my turn to console her.

The next day, I got a call from the casting director on *Philadelphia* to do a table reading for the part of Tom Hanks's character's boyfriend, and my hopes soared. I drove to Columbia Pictures and went into a room where the producers and the director, Jonathan Demme, were all sitting around a huge table. Even though I was nervous, when I saw the scene in the script that I had to read I almost laughed out loud: Tom Hanks's character and the boyfriend go to a costume party as . . . wait for it . . . Desi and Lucy. I pulled out all the stops during my audition and did my best Desi, and they loved it, laughing and smiling.

As I was leaving, Demme piped up, "I like you." He smiled.

I left on a high, waiting for word from my agent about the part, and in the morning he called and said they loved me. But words in Hollywood are often false. Nothing happened, then a week went by, followed by a month, then another. I had given up on the role, so I was surprised when my agent called several months later and said I was in second position.

"Who's in first?" I pressed.

"Antonio Banderas," he answered. I knew of the relatively unknown actor. "If he passes, you're it," my agent promised.

Again I waited for the call, but when it finally came, it wasn't good news.

"Banderas took the part."

I was devastated. It's almost harder to be so close to getting the job than having no chance at all. My bigger problem was debt, because I was thirty thousand dollars in the hole and couldn't seem to get ahead. After two years in Los Angeles, I felt like my life was going nowhere.

At the end of my rope, I decided to give it one more shot when my agent told me I had gotten an audition for an independent Italian movie I wanted to be in more than anything. I ran lines with Paula for hours, memorizing them, desperate to make it happen, and had a hard time sleeping that night. The next day, when I walked in, I started saying the lines I'd memorized and the director immediately interrupted me.

"We didn't call you in for that part," he said, staring at me, irritated.

It was terribly awkward and I was mortified. Surprisingly, he asked if I could learn the other part in five minutes, so I studied it and went back in, but I didn't do well and left quickly in a state of despair. At home, I couldn't let it go and pestered my agent until he promised he could get me back in for another audition. He managed to get the director to agree to see me again, but I had gotten no sleep and the stress of the past two years was taking me down to that familiar dark place, so when I did the scene, I was way too into it. I had a meltdown and couldn't stop weeping, and the producers were so worried they didn't know what to do. Should they call 911? I knew I had blown it, and so did my agent when they asked him if I was mentally unstable. That was it—I was ready to let go of my dream, I didn't have any more to give and I was going to walk the hell away from acting.

But a few hours later, just as I decided there was no future for me in Los Angeles, the producers of the long-running daytime serial *General Hospital* called. They liked my work on *All My Children* and wanted me to come to the ABC Prospect Studios to read for them. I was tired of the emotional roller coaster I had been on as a freelance actor but promised Paula I would go read for the part, so she drove me to the meeting and sat outside in the parking lot anxiously while I read for Wendy Riche, who had just taken over as executive producer a year before, and Shelley Curtis, who had also just returned to the show as producer. They both loved my reading, we talked for three hours, and by the time the meeting was over they had offered me a job.

I had to choose between two roles: Damian Smith, a mobster, and Michael "Sonny" Corinthos, Jr., a character who ran a strip club. Sonny was only a six-month arc, but I liked the name Sonny and I liked that it was a short contract. And that was how Sonny came to be; I would take him from the page and create him from scratch. Just like that, after all the could've, should've, would've moments, the lost roles, the frustration, my life changed . . . in more ways than one.

The darkness that I couldn't escape had found me again, and this time it was threatening to destroy everything I had worked so hard to attain.

CHAPTER EIGHT

Man in the Mirror

In August 1993, my first day at *General Hospital* was Friday the thirteenth, and maybe I should have taken that as an ominous sign.

The show started at seven a.m. and Paula drove me to the ABC Prospect Studios in Franklin Hills, entering through the gate for cast members and making our way to the reserved parking. It occurred to me as I walked to the main door that the building actually looked like a hospital from the exterior.

On the way to my dressing room, the very first person I saw was the actor who plays Scott Baldwin in the fictional town of Port Charles.

"Hi, I'm Kin Shriner," he greeted me warmly. I'll never forget what he said next. "Don't let anyone screw around with your character."

I didn't realize it at first and wouldn't know until we became friends, but Kin suffers from OCD. Obsessive-compulsive disorder is a chronic disorder in which a person has uncontrollable, obsessive thoughts and compulsive behaviors and feels the need to repeat them over and over. In the movies it's often depicted as quirky or even comical that someone has a fear of germs and must have things in symmetrical order, but OCD is not humorous and can also expand to aggressive thoughts toward self or others involving sex, religion, and harm.

When eventually Kin shared with me that he had dealt with OCD his whole life, I realized we had something more than the show in common, because OCD causes anxiety for the person who has the disorder. Many who suffer from it also experience depression and may use alcohol or drugs to ease the anxiety or depression. It can really disrupt work and life but can be treated with medication, psychotherapy, or a combination of the two. Despite not knowing about our common experience when we met, I felt an instant connection—one that would only grow over time.

After meeting Kin, I wound my way through the maze of hallways that also resembled a hospital, with that neutral tone and fluorescent lighting that makes you lose your sense of time and place, past the greenroom where extras were getting coffee and looking at lines. I found the makeup department next to wardrobe, where the costume designer had already done fittings and selected Sonny's signature wardrobe for me the week before.

After I sat for hair and makeup, I waited to be called upstairs to the set, and when I heard my named on the PA system, I started up the stairs. I walked through the maze of dark sets to the facade where Sonny did most of his business at that time: a strip club named the Paradise Lounge. I felt uneasy, and considering I had been hanging out at strip clubs and lying to Paula about it for months, walking into another strip joint put my mind in a dark place. My first day I was also filled with anxiety and felt an enormous amount of pressure because I had several monologues and knew I couldn't forget any lines or the pressure would be even greater. Although I didn't work with Tony Geary or Genie Francis much at first, I couldn't believe I watched Luke and Laura in high school and now here I was on the same show. I had also told Wendy Riche when I accepted the job that I had one caveat—I didn't want anyone telling me I had to talk louder because I wanted to be subtle and to bring more of a movie style of acting to the table. As the crew adjusted the lights and we began blocking and rehearsing, suddenly the director, Joe Behar, stopped me.

"Maurice, can you please speak a little louder?"

I bristled and continued to speak at the volume I had been speaking, repeating the line and continuing the scene, but Joe stopped it again.

"Maurice, we still can't hear you, can you do it again? Louder, please."

I did the scene again but never raised my voice, and finally the director moved on. I fought that particular battle for a while and they finally stopped asking me to raise my voice.

I wanted Sonny to be a combination of traits from characters I had liked growing up: questioning and strategic like Columbo; cool like Billy Jack; quietly powerful like Michael Corleone in *The Godfather*; and Jimmy Doyle in *New York, New York*. These guys all had an intensity about them because they would, at any cost, take you down to get to the truth. I also decided to infuse Sonny with a little-boy quality, to counter the danger that is obvious. I never wanted anything for Sonny that wasn't truthful.

It was exhausting, however, to make him likable, because in the beginning he wasn't even remotely a nice guy, he was mean and he did despicable things. The story line at the time involved Sonny taking in a sixteen-year-old named Karen, played by the lovely and talented Cari Shayne, giving her drugs, and having sex with her. Like I said, Sonny was bad in those days. He's nicer now, but I think fans like the character so much and allowed him to get away with so many things over the years because life is hard, and sometimes you want bad people to pay—and Sonny will make them pay. He might have done some horrible things himself—which I'm not excusing—but he was also fiercely loyal and would do anything to defend the people he loved.

Although the world was enamored with the new face in Port Charles and the network was pleased with me, Paula started to notice something was off after a week. I walked around the house and played Michael Jackson's song "Man in the Mirror" over and over. I thought I had a unique connection to Michael Jackson because, off my meds, my mind convinced me Michael Jackson was singing about me *to* me. Every time I played it Paula got a knot in her stomach, and she still hates that song. She knew something was wrong but figured I would adjust to the new show and my outlook would improve. When I had gone off lithium the last time, I hadn't gotten violent, it had been more of a religious experience. Paula had not been around for the mental institution and my first breakdown, so she no idea what was in store for us in the coming days.

Neither did the producers of *General Hospital*. No one knew I was bipolar because it was long before it was okay to admit things like that, particularly for guys—and particularly a guy playing a tough guy on a TV show. No one knew I was starting a downward spiral, not even me. I was hiding it from myself just as well as I hid it from everyone else. At work, in my dressing room, I had put up a poster of Al Pacino and every day I listened to "The Godfather" soundtrack over and over before scenes because I wanted to become Sonny, and not in a good way.

It was only about two weeks in on *General Hospital* that I began hearing voices when no one was in the room with me. I heard them on set, in the car, and at home. They were everywhere and they were telling me I had to find out the truth, no matter what the cost. They were saying the truth would set everyone free.

At the end of the two weeks, I was completely delusional. Since I'm a method actor, the people at work thought I was just really into the role. At home, I began behaving like my character, and as I said, Sonny was meaner then, tough and lethal.

One night during a conversation Paula asked me, "Honey, why are you saying the lines we ran last night?"

"What do you mean?" I asked.

"You're saying the lines we ran. That's what Sonny said."

I just shrugged it off, but Paula was worried for several reasons—most importantly because we had tiny guests. Although Paula still barely spoke to her mother, and wouldn't step foot in her house, she wanted to help the little girls who were stuck there like she had been. So Paula often brought them to our house for long spans of time.

The timing couldn't have been worse.

That night, the voices were at a crescendo, telling me I had to confess all my sins to Paula. When I did, it was like a cleansing; I was twitching and crying and my secrets came out in a heated, jumbled, emotional rush. I told her about going to the strip clubs, and falling for one of the dancers, that I had slept with a girl in San Francisco, and that I had tried to sleep with Kelly in Hawaii. Paula was mad, but she was also crying because she was so frightened. I was in a hyper-manic state and I was just getting started. I grabbed a bottle of wine and drank the entire contents right out of the bottle before throwing it at her and yelling at her to stop crying. I was beyond drunk at this point and held her toy poodle, Nyco, up over my head and said I would kill him.

Somehow, Paula talked me out of that, but I continued to drink. The more I drank, the bigger the bravado and the scarier I became. I boasted how I was fine without my medicine and didn't really need to ever take it again. Paula knew I had stopped my lithium but at the time she didn't know any better and didn't insist that I take it. She thought I was okay—until she saw I wasn't.

I heard a banging at that point and realized it was Paula's knees shaking. Along with fearing for her own safety, Vanessa and Angie, who weren't more than five, were asleep in the bed. As I bounced around the house in a manic rage I went in their room and Paula followed, panicked, and as she came down the hallway she saw me standing over them, saying it would be easy to kill them. Paula begged and pleaded for me to stop and eventually I bounced around the house some more.

I put on "Man in the Mirror" at full volume and started singing it at the top of my lungs; I was convinced Michael Jackson was on his way over in a limo to save me. When I went into the other room, I slapped my dog Corleone, before beginning to cry uncontrollably. Paula seized this opportunity to grab her nieces and run across the street with them. She didn't know the neighbors, but knocked on the door and begged them to let the girls stay there. She knew she only had a moment before I would realize she was gone, and she told the neighbors she would explain later. Although Paula was scared, she knew I probably would get more violent if she didn't return, and, God forbid, if the cops showed up violence would definitely take place. I asked her later why she came back and I'll never forget what she told me.

She looked at me lovingly and said, "Babe, I knew the maniacal guy in my living room making threats wasn't my husband. I knew your illness had taken you hostage and, somewhere inside, the real you was still there. I had no doubt and I was going to get him back."

I'm the luckiest guy in the world. If Paula hadn't come back, who knows what I would have done, but I'd probably be dead.

That night, Paula was on a mission to save not just her nieces or herself from harm, but to save me. She was as determined as she was desperate, grasping at anything that might help. Since the last breakdown had involved me talking to God, she thought the brother of a friend of mine from my modeling days in San Francisco, Vinnie Vanni, might be able to talk me down. He was religious and could quote entire Bible verses and if he could attempt an exorcism maybe that would work. She was willing to try anything. Although Vinnie did his best over the phone, it had no effect on me and only made me more belligerent, but Paula sat with me, hoping I would calm down and not hurt her. I continued to drink and eye Paula as if she were the enemy, and rambled incoherently for some time. At one point I threatened to kill Paula, but as I raged and hovered over her, she stayed, despite her fear, trying to talk me down.

Eventually I dozed off, and that gave Paula a chance to call Dr. Noonan, the doctor in San Francisco who had diagnosed me with bipolar disorder. She told him what was happening and begged for his help and Dr. Noonan called in a prescription for a tranquilizer. After Paula ran to the drugstore to pick it up, once again she risked returning to the house, and when she entered, I had woken up and was waiting with a broken bottle. She ran into another room and called Danny, pleading with him to come help her get me to take the medication. That would be much easier said than done, because that night I thought I was a messiah and wanted total truth from all beings. When Danny arrived, I agreed to take the tranquilizer but I insisted first we had to go to Danny's house.

"Let's confront the devil!" I yelled.

It was the middle of the night and his wife would be asleep, so they tried to talk me out of my demand, but I wasn't swayed. When they realized they couldn't dissuade me from my mission of truth, Paula and Danny went with me, and once we got to Danny's house I ran inside before Danny could stop me. I leapt up the stairs two steps at a time, until I burst through his wife's bedroom door. She woke up, startled, and when she saw me, wild-eyed, she screamed.

"Do you believe in God?" I asked her as she jumped out of bed. "You sold your soul to the devil!" I continued yelling at her as she barricaded herself in the bathroom.

I was making no sense, out of my mind with mania, and she screamed at me to leave, but I didn't, I continued instead to hurl accusations through the door.

By this time Danny had gotten to the bedroom and was trying to pull me away from the door, but it got worse and I started yelling, "Devil get out!" as if I were trying to cast a demon from her. After a struggle, he somehow got me out of the house, but I was screaming the whole way. I finally calmed down a little once we got to the car, but I refused to get in and insisted I was returning home on foot, so Paula and Danny had no choice but to watch me walk away into the darkness.

On the way home, I passed a Catholic church and decided to go inside, but as I entered, in my manic state, wearing dirty sweats and seemingly indigent, the priest stopped me, telling me I couldn't come in the church dressed like that. Troubled, and wandering back into the dark alone, I decided to leave the Catholic Church for good.

By the time I got back home, Paula and Danny were waiting for me and I was so exhausted I agreed to take the tranquilizer, and finally went to sleep. The next day, the deep, dark depression hit and I wouldn't go out of my room, and Paula had to make the call to my brand-new employers at *General Hospital* to tell them I was sick and needed a week or two off from the show. In soap time, it was like asking for a year, because the story lines were dense and intertwined and being gone required huge scheduling changes that impacted everyone and everything.

We were both terrified this might be the end of my new job, but Paula made the call and explained that something was terribly wrong with me and she was talking to a psychiatrist and would update them. Instead of cutting their losses and firing me, the producers stood by me, and as Paula continued to update them, they made it work with the show's story line, rescheduling everything so I could be absent from Port Charles.

Meanwhile, Paula sent me to a psychiatrist down the street that we could walk to, but I scared him the very first session when he tried to ask me questions.

"Fuck you, motherfucker, don't fuck with me!" I screamed, and jumped at him.

Paula took control and made me sit down, but I knew the doctor was terrified and that emboldened me. It was very tense and I resisted his help, although I did take the medication he prescribed to knock me out that first day, and somehow Paula convinced me to start taking my lithium again.

After two weeks of going to therapy daily, and the medicine

getting back into my system to even out my mania, I had to face the real world, and that meant returning to the set. It was the hardest thing I had ever done in my life. It was difficult being the new guy on the show, and now on top of that I had no confidence, was depressed, and didn't have a confidant there who I could talk to or who I felt would understand.

My first day back I walked onto the strip joint set and had to do a scene where Karen tells Sonny her father abused her. It hit way too close to home and I began tearing up, remembering my father hitting me. I couldn't control my emotions or the tears, but I needed to because I was the bad guy. No matter how hard I tried, I was too fragile to do it, and I couldn't stop crying or finish the scene. I finally had to leave the set, and I was sitting on the couch in my dressing room, still crying, when Shelley Curtis knocked on the door and came in. She sat on the couch next to me and patiently listened.

"I don't know how I'm going to get through this," I told her.

She looked at me and said, "You can do it," and I could tell she believed that.

"I don't think I can."

But she wouldn't give up on me and I will never forget what she told me next. "We will take it page by page, line by line, word by word if we have to," she said as she hugged me.

This time, unlike my experiences after the first breakdowns, the pressures were enormous because the show was my livelihood; my future as an actor depended on me showing up every day. Millions of people were watching me as I healed, without even knowing what I was struggling to overcome. It was the lowest point in my life, next to being in the mental institution, but even though I wanted to quit *General Hospital*, Shelley and

Wendy convinced me to stay and worked with me so I could recover and rebound.

These two incredible strangers who hired me were giving me a second chance, and they still believed in me even when they didn't have to and probably had good reason not to. They had just taken over the show and were facing enormous pressure as well—they were going in a bold new direction and nothing was as bold as keeping me on and betting on me. I wanted to show them they weren't wrong and I could deliver what they had seen in me that first day we met. They were the most gracious and kind producers in the world and that is something for which I will always be grateful.

Although it was initially only a six-month arc for my character, Sonny's popularity exploded almost overnight, and they asked if I could continue in the role and extend the six months to a year.

I agreed, and then my real journey began.

CHAPTER NINE

Sweet Child o' Mine

When I met the great Anthony "Tony" Geary, who played Luke Spencer, I knew immediately there was something unique about him—a gravitas both men and women love. Our characters became partners in crime on the show, and we became dear friends off-screen, but let me just say he scared the hell out of me initially.

The first time I had to do a scene with him I was literally shaking. We were on the stairs to Luke's house and the script called for him to grab me. Well, when we got to that part of the scene, he grabbed me so hard, with so much force and power from his character, I was so in the moment as Sonny that I pushed back just as forcefully and ad-libbed to get his damn hands off me. Tony told me later shooting that scene was when I gained his respect.

As we started to work together, I also got to know Genie Francis, who played Luke's soul mate, Laura. Their chemistry was pure magic, and I always respected her talent—subtly layered and full of emotion. She's also one of the kindest, sweetest people I know, and just like Tony, she wound up being a close friend.

It was actually Tony who brought up the idea of a life for

Sonny outside of crime when he asked one day, "Hey, Maurice, do you want to just be Tonto to my Lone Ranger?"

I weighed the question before answering honestly. "Tony, I enjoy working with you a lot. But, yes, I'd love to do my own thing."

He winked. "Then go upstairs and ask them for a family."

I then told the writer and producer Claire Labine that I was happy doing the show, but that I would like for Sonny to have a fuller, more rounded character life—and if they couldn't accommodate that, I understood. Of course, throughout that conversation I knew they were also aware that my contract was coming up for negotiation, which gave me an edge.

That's when Sonny finally got a life. First Claire gave him a girlfriend. Vanessa Marcil, who originated the popular role of Brenda, had been on the show a year before I arrived.

From the minute we both touched the same suitcase on the dock after they put us in a scene together, it was inevitable. Fans ate it up and we became an on-screen couple. I loved working with her. Off-screen, I asked her one day if she wanted to be a good actress or a great actress.

Of course she wanted to be great and accepted my challenge to work her ass off. Which she did. She was like a sponge and wanted me to teach her everything I knew about method acting.

Around the same time I saw a scene with Steve Burton, who plays Jason Morgan, and told the writers his talent was wasted. I asked them to write a story line for us and they put Jason in a terrible car accident, after which he forgot he was a Quartermaine and came to work for Sonny. The minute we did a scene another great fan favorite was born—Sonny and Jason are like Batman and Robin, they need each other. We started working together all the time and it wasn't long after that when I gave Steve the same challenge that I had given Vanessa about acting.

"You're deep and you've got talent, but it's wasted. You want me to help you out? You want me to teach you the method?" I asked him one day at work.

Like Vanessa, he was all in. We went over scenes in my dressing room; sometimes he came to my house, where we worked for hours. On set, he took intensity to a new level and started being intense even while pouring a cup of coffee, which got the attention of the director.

"Steve, what are you doing?" the director asked.

"Maurice is teaching me the method."

The director groaned. "Okay, Steve, I get it. Maurice's acting method is great. *But you're pouring a cup of coffee.*"

Everyone erupted into laughter, including Steve.

I was happy, too. At last I was bringing in money and could support my family without taking any more funds from my father. When I found out in the summer that I was going to be a father myself, that added a whole other layer of excitement. Paula, of course, was over the moon, and while I was thrilled, I also felt overwhelmed by emotion. It was exciting and a little terrifying to think about being responsible for a little human being—and it made me even more aware of my responsibility to myself, and to Paula. I had vowed to her I'd never go off my meds again, and now staying on lithium became more important than ever.

With the big upcoming change, the time felt right to buy a home. Paula found a beautiful rustic-wood-style house nestled off Cahuenga Boulevard on North Knoll Drive with enough property to eventually build a barn for the horses Paula always dreamed of owning and the pool I had always wanted. It reminded me of homes in Montana—big wood beams, open space, and lots of windows looking out on a gorgeous private view. There was plenty of space for what we would affectionately call Paula's Ark—every animal in need would eventually find its way to her.

Once we had the keys to the property, life seemed so perfect because we had everything we could possibly want. We didn't know the sex of the baby but we were excited either way, and Paula set about getting the nursery ready to welcome the new addition to our family. She had big beautiful murals painted on the walls from a Precious Moments calendar she loved and the focal point of the mural was a little girl praying, because religion had been a refuge for Paula herself as a little girl—she always says it saved her life.

Our perfect world was shattered around Thanksgiving when we attended a movie screening. While I schmoozed with people at the after-party, Paula disappeared into the bathroom. A few moments later when she emerged, her face was completely white and I knew something was terribly wrong. She told me she was hemorrhaging, so I immediately took her straight to the hospital. The whole way there we both prayed that everything would be all right, but I had a bad feeling.

Once the doctor examined her, they gave us the bad news— Paula had lost the baby and had to stay in the hospital over the holiday to undergo a D&C. We were shocked and heartbroken. I couldn't stop thinking about all the what-ifs and all that would never be. Neither of us could bring ourselves to go into the nursery. We just kept the door closed.

That year, we didn't even decorate the house for Christmas. We were still grieving and processing our pain when we were blessed with a miracle in the New Year. It was in January that Paula announced that she was pregnant again.

Our world had crashed and soared, all within a matter of weeks. This time, Paula was a nervous wreck, worrying about every detail. She stopped coloring her hair, drinking soda, or doing anything that might even remotely have a negative impact on the baby.

It didn't help our fears that right after she found out she was pregnant the January 17, 1994, Northridge earthquake struck. We were in bed when we heard a thundering rumble and terrifying roar as everything started shaking. I instinctively threw myself across Paula's belly to protect our unborn child. It was suddenly pitch-black—the electricity went out almost everywhere, which is eerie in a big city because there's always some source of light somewhere. It was so dark I could actually see the stars, and it felt like the world was ending.

What sounded like a million car alarms began wailing in the night. We could hear everything in the house breaking, as the TV, the dishes, all Paula's beloved Swarovski crystal, and everything in the cabinets was flung across the rooms by Mother Nature's powerful unseen hand. When the shaking stopped, the sound of neighbors' voices far away drifted toward us as they ran out of their homes. Once I knew Paula was all right, we ran out into the backyard, too, afraid that the dogs were crushed under a fifty-foot brick wall that had toppled like a kid's building blocks. We were relieved when we found them hiding in the garage.

But the aftershocks were just as unnerving and unpredictable as the earthquake. They kept going on for days, keeping everything swaying and the whole city on edge. Every time another one hit, we prayed that the baby was okay, and after several days, when things finally calmed down and the earth seemed to feel solid again, we were grateful that we were all safe and the house was structurally intact. So many people were less fortunate than we were.

To keep myself distracted from everything that could go wrong before the baby came, I kept pushing myself professionally. Even though I had gotten the role of Sonny, could call myself a working actor, and was becoming a household name, I couldn't sit on my laurels. I had always had my sights set on becoming a member of the Actors Studio, and despite having not yet been asked to join the prestigious and small club, I was determined to go back and audition.

I chose a scene from *American Buffalo*, which I studied and practiced for weeks. When I walked into the small theater, I saw the judges: successful industry veterans Shelley Winters, Mark Rydell, and Martin Landau, who patiently waited as I took a deep breath, steadied my thoughts, and finally launched into my scene. I felt the electricity in the room and the judges seemed enthralled with the performance, but by now I knew you could never tell with auditions. You can overthink and second-guess yourself all you want, but when it comes down to it, you still always just have to wait for the call.

Talk about anxiety, though; it was incredible to even be in the company of such talent. The Actors Studio had only admitted around eight hundred members since it was founded in 1947, including actors I respect such as Al Pacino, Marlon Brando, Dustin Hoffman, Robert De Niro, Christopher Walken, and Paul Newman, actors I had watched in movies growing up and whose skills I wanted to emulate.

Luckily, my instincts were correct and I was given high marks for my audition. Before I could become a member, however, there were still more hurdles to overcome. For the next year I was required to attend sessions at the Actors Studio, and at the end of that time I would then have to audition again. If I did well and they thought I had what it took to join the ranks of the chosen few, they would extend an invitation to the club.

I was focused on more than professional growth, though. The whole year of attending sessions in L.A., I was also going to therapy, which was a powerful tool I realized I had to use consistently in my life, along with taking my meds. In particular, I was working on my deep-seated childhood anger and the unresolved issues with my father. The story line about abuse at *General Hospital* had stayed with me and forced me to deal with it once and for all.

I told H.J. I had held on to rage all these years from being hit by our father, but my brother didn't understand why I was so upset. He had gotten hit, too, but he didn't think it was that bad. I wonder if he just pushed it somewhere out of his consciousness, or maybe I was just the sensitive kid. But I kept obsessing over it and one day when I was discussing it with my therapist—as I had done for months—my therapist told me there was only one move to make.

I had to confront my father in order to move past this.

It took me a few weeks to wrap my head around that and work up the nerve, but I finally did and sat my father down with my mom.

"I want to talk to you," I began with such a serious tone that he and my mother exchanged worried looks, and then I took a deep breath. This was it, there was no turning back. "I want to understand why I was hit so much, I want to know why was I abused," I said.

My father was completely caught off guard, and so was my mother.

"I didn't abuse you," my father said, stunned.

"It hurt me, I felt abused," I said firmly, and my mother had tears in her eyes as I continued, "You don't know what it's like as a little boy looking up at a six-foot-tall man who is full of anger. You don't know how it feels to wait for that to happen, for that anxiety to build. I remember your footsteps, and the door opening, and that moment before you hit me is almost as bad as the belt cutting into me."

My father sat there for the longest time, and then he looked me in the eye and opened up a little. "My father hit me all the time. His father hit him, and his father hit him before that. It's the way it always was," he said, not understanding. "And your brother didn't seem to have a problem with it, he didn't turn out like you."

"H.J. wasn't as sensitive as I was," I said, standing my ground. "Dad, you can have five kids and do exactly the same thing, and if one of them has a precondition, it's going to make that child have a problem even if the others don't. But that's not all, you always wanted everything to be perfect, but nothing's perfect. Nothing. No matter how hard you try, something will always disappoint you, someone will always fall short."

When I finally stopped arguing my passionate case I waited anxiously for my father's response.

For the first time, he looked at me like he finally saw that little boy who was afraid of him, and he softened. "I'm sorry, Mauricio," he finally said, and I really believed that he meant it.

It was such a departure from the tough image I had grown up with that it took me aback, but in that instant I felt so much love for my father. It helped me tremendously to hear those words. As I watched him making an effort to bridge the gap between us, I softened, too. I just wish I had told him how I felt sooner.

"I know it's what your father did to you, and his father to him, and it's all you knew," I told him.

I think that was the first time we really understood each other, and our relationship started improving after that. I'm grateful it has evolved as I have.

Now that I was at peace with my father, the role of my life—fatherhood—was imminent. Shelley Curtis threw Paula a beautiful baby shower at her home. Vanessa, Wendy, and two of the show's other producers, Carol Scott and Chris Magarian, attended to show Paula the love she so deserved. It meant so much that Shelley opened her home to Paula and truly made her feel like she was family. I think Paula talked about that shower for a week straight after it had happened. It goes to show how much these beautiful, powerful women have been such a strong influence on our lives, and I will forever be grateful to them.

Paula's due date came and went without Paula going into labor. Another day passed. Then a week. I had waited nervously before, but now the anticipation was causing my anxiety to spike through the roof. While I was at work, Paula went to her obstetrician, Dr. Paul Crane (who delivered all of the Kardashians and Beyoncé's babies), every day to have the baby checked and to see if Paula had dilated.

A full two weeks after her due date, which seemed like a thousand years, Dr. Crane told Paula her amniotic fluid was dangerously low. Memories of the first miscarriage haunted us and Dr. Crane advised us for the baby's safety to induce labor.

We chose that Sunday. When the weekend finally arrived, our plan went off flawlessly: I drove Paula to the hospital, got her settled in her room, and things seemed fine. However, an hour after we got there, the baby's heart stopped, and suddenly the Code Blue alarm sounded. As the hospital staff rushed to Paula's room, I stood there in the chaos fearing the worst. I prayed for a miracle, and after several tense moments Dr. Crane stabilized the baby's heart and Paula and I locked eyes, grateful but still frightened because it wasn't over yet. He then prepped Paula for an emergency C-section, administering an epidural, and we waited. After a few tense hours, fortunately the baby's vitals settled and we were able to wait for Paula to dilate and deliver without the procedure.

But we were still nervous, so in the delivery room I tried to keep things light by talking to Dr. Crane, whose son also happened to be an actor, about his favorite actors—in between instructing Paula to push.

"Jack Nicholson, right?" he told me, then turned back to Paula. "Paula, push . . ."

I nodded. "Right! In *One Flew Over the Cuckoo's Nest*." We discussed a scene and laughed.

"Paula, puuuuusssssshhhh," Dr. Crane told her again. "She's almost there," he said, then went back to discussing another actor.

Finally, after about two hours, on September 18, 1994, Cailey Sofia Benard decided to enter the world, and when we heard her first cry, I stepped into the real-world role of father. Paula, too, stepped into the role she was born to take on, motherhood, and finally had the one precious thing she had wanted most since she herself was a child: a real family.

Looking down at the bundle in my arms, I couldn't remember any of the reasons I had waited to have kids. Once I saw the little girl, *my little girl*, with her full head of black hair and her perfect face and tiny hands that grabbed onto mine, I was hopelessly hooked.

Paula and I both had tears in our eyes as I cut the umbilical cord. It was nothing like I had ever felt before; it was surreal and amazing and overwhelming. You look at this tiny little being you know is now depending on you for everything. You know you have to take care of her and you suddenly feel this deep, natural instinct in your gut to protect her and you realize you will do anything for her.

After my daughter was born, fatherhood became the number-one priority in my life and it's apt that I received that most meaningful trophy before I ever got an Emmy statue. Paula's priority was giving our daughter the stability she had never had. Our child was never going to feel unloved, unwanted. She would never have to live in survival mode.

Paula had needed to escape her bad home situation as a child, and being a mother herself made her realize not just how she wanted to raise her child, but also that she wanted to repair the relationship with her own mother. So she started the slow, painful process.

While I was enjoying my newfound fatherhood, at work another one of my favorite story lines was unfolding: one in which Sonny loses an unborn child. Sonny's doomed marriage to Lily, played by Lilly Melgar, who's fantastic, had a real beginning, a real middle, and a great ending, because in those days story lines lasted for months. When Lily died, she was blown up by a car bomb meant for Sonny.

Because her death was so traumatizing for everyone, it made the scene later, when Lily came to Sonny in a dream with their baby, all the more powerful. It was a particularly emotional scene for me because my little girl Cailey, our amazing gift after losing our own unborn baby, was playing Sonny's unborn son.

After the birth of my child, I also finally got my own family on *General Hospital* when, in 1995, Mike came to Port Charles and the audience found out he was Sonny's father. Mike was a grifter and I had the privilege to work on their deliciously difficult father-son relationship in scenes with the great Ron Hale.

But what I remember most fondly about working with Ron actually happened outside the show.

While I had been attending the Actors Studio that year, I never had the nerve to put up a scene because I couldn't bring myself to put myself out there like that in front of people I admired and respected so much. When it was time to audition for the Actors Studio again, I decided to do a scene from *I Never Sang for My Father*, a Gene Hackman movie based on the play.

The character I played was an angry son, which was interesting, in that I had gone through a similar journey with my own father. It required a scene partner, someone to play the father, so I asked Ron to step into that role. Performing the scene was nerve-racking, but it was an intense private tension I was learning to use professionally. The scene was charged and emotional between a father and the son who blames him for the death of his mother. I knew that Ron would connect to it on a personal level, and this, along with my own catharsis with my father, heightened the level of our emotions and we blew the scene out of the water.

For once, there was no agonizing wait. I achieved a lifelong dream when I was congratulated on my performance and invited to become a member. They were so impressed they also asked Ron to join. That day is one of those sweet moments in life you relish.

I achieved another step toward another dream in 1996, when Cailey was two, only three years after taking the role on *General Hospital*, when I was nominated for my first Emmy Award. I was so happy. At the time, Sonny had been going through a wrenching and critically acclaimed emotional story line that centered around his teenage friend Stone and Stone's girlfriend, Robin, facing his AIDS diagnosis, decline, and death at only nineteen with passion and dignity. It was one of the best story lines I've ever been a part of and I'm still proud of the writing, the performances, and the directing; all of it was just superb. It will always be at the top of my list of favorite story arcs.

I of course had watched Kimberly McCullough, who plays Robin Scorpio, pretty much grow up on the show and love her on stage and off. Scenes in that AIDS story line with her were powerful and intense and emotionally draining and she really held her own. The other amazing actor I worked with in the story was Michael Sutton, who played Stone Cates. Once Michael knew his character was going to die within a year's time on the show, he came to me and asked me to work with him. We rehearsed relentlessly and he was also a sponge about learning method acting. His hard work paid off when he was nominated for an Emmy, as was Kimberly.

My first nomination was more exciting than I ever could have imagined and I felt that finally my years of hard work were being recognized. My friends and family who believed in me would be thrilled, and my friends and family who doubted me would finally have to admit I had chosen the right path. Back then, the Emmy ceremony took place at Radio City Music Hall and we attended the show in New York dressed to the nines, but I had to be escorted everywhere by six or seven armed undercover cops because crowds swarmed and people grabbed at me any way they could, holding on to my arms, my head, my ass, anything.

In New York, it's like Sonny's the mayor, and crowds still stop me on the streets all the time. The beauty of the *General Hospital* fans is how loyal they are; even though I didn't win that first year, it still felt amazing.

It felt like being a rock star.

CHAPTER TEN

Isn't She Lovely

It wasn't all about my career in those days . . . but it sure was taking off. Back then, Brenda and Sonny were the hot couple, and fans couldn't get enough of them.

The on-screen chemistry was undeniable, truly once-in-a-lifetime. A fan recently put a link to an early episode with Sonny and Brenda on my Twitter account and I couldn't stop watching it because the heat was amazing. To keep up with the fans' rabid interest in the super-couple, we were doing three or four loves scenes a week. It was ridiculous, but I didn't want to look like a wuss, so I didn't say anything. Paula didn't want me to just be branded a "soap hunk" and we argued all the time about that because my ego wouldn't allow me to admit to myself—or to Paula—that she was right.

I needed to stand up for myself and tell the producers that I was a serious actor and wanted a story line to show that. Vanessa understood and didn't take it personally, because she and Paula had become very close. They both wanted the story line to have more depth. Vanessa always teases me that Paula should have married *her*.

At home, my talkative daughter Cailey was four and her strong will and wicked intelligence (as well as sense of humor) had already infused our family dynamic. Like Paula, she was obsessed with animals, and loved the fun birthday parties Paula always put together, which usually featured a petting zoo.

Cailey has also always been fascinated with snakes, just like me, and from the time she was little she wanted to hold any snake she saw . . . which is fine if they're not poisonous. One afternoon I'll never forget, Cailey and I were in the car and we were both in shock when we saw a five-and-a-half-foot rattlesnake slithering in the middle of the road. I got out to check it out, but I made Cailey stay in the car, although she really wanted to get out and see the snake up close.

Once I was closer and realized it wasn't a rattlesnake I didn't let on, instead I put on quite a show for Cailey, wrestling with the snake and finally capturing it. Cailey's eyes were as big as the moon, and I was the hero—until we called Paula and she informed Cailey I was teasing her, because of course it wasn't a rattlesnake.

In 1997, Brenda and Sonny were finally engaged and the fans were in a frenzy. It was also wonderful to be acknowledged again with another Emmy nomination; however, by this time I had developed a love/hate relationship with the soap and my character. It afforded me a great life and I could provide for my wife and baby girl, but I wanted to see what else was out there and, as I had done before with *All My Children*, I told the producers I wanted to leave when my contract expired in a year. The producers didn't want to kill off the popular character, and they wrote Sonny out of the show by having him leave Brenda at the altar so Sonny could return at a later date if I ever wanted to come back to Port Charles.

That goodbye episode was incredible, but the fans were

devastated. I remember sitting in the limo for a nine-page scene with Steve Burton that we had rehearsed the hell out of before shooting—and that day did it in one take. He was brilliant and I was so proud of him and let him know that. The raw acting and emotion were amazing, and when he won an Emmy, I've never seen a better Emmy tape with better performance clips.

After I finished my last day, Wendy and Shelley threw a nice going-away party for me with a big cake, and when I walked in I could hear a song playing. "Sunny, thank you for the sunshine bouquet, Sunny, thank you for the I love you brought my way. . . . Sunny, one so true, I love you." People told stories and shook my hand and wished me well.

When one of the makeup artists came up to me during the party I was surprised when we both almost started to cry. Donna Messina was the matriarch of *General Hospital* and had been there for years, but she wasn't my makeup artist at that time and I didn't know her well. She was notorious for not liking hugs and yet she hugged me and, standing there, in that short period of time at the party, we connected. It was the beginning of an amazing friendship.

Before I ever considered returning to Port Charles, I had to see what other territories there were to conquer. Right after quitting, I hired a hot young manager who promised me the moon. I did some independent movies, including *Operation Splitsville* as Frank, and *Restraining Order* as Sicko, with Eric Roberts.

Meanwhile, Paula had continued her quest to foster a better relationship with her mother. Now that they were speaking, Paula started trying to get Heather, now five, out of the same house her mother still lived in with Paula's other siblings and all the drug addicts. Although her contact with her mother was still minimal,

Paula started bringing Heather to stay with us during the summer and she was a lot of fun to have around. Heather was so adorable; she looked like a little Diana Ross, and I always loved to mess with her, claiming, "Your mama can't cook!" and in this little high, defiant voice, she always replied, "She can, too, cook!" but I just kept repeating it and she kept on arguing with me. She and Cailey were less than two years apart and loved playing together and they became fast friends, growing very close.

During my hiatus from the show, Sonny might not have been on TV but he was definitely not forgotten. One memorable day I got a call from Eddie DeBartolo, Jr.'s daughter, who was a huge fan of Sonny and all things Port Charles. She asked if I wanted to come to a game, which she could arrange because her father, Eddie, owned the 49ers. Who would say no to that?

She took me into the owner's box at Candlestick Park where Sean Penn, Jessica Lange, Jason Priestley, and a few others were already seated. Halftime, when we went out on the field to stand on the sidelines and watch, is most memorable for me. Cops had to escort us because the fans were so intense and I'll never forget, as I walked onto the grass, that part of the stadium started chanting:

"Sonny! Sonny!"

Then it got slightly louder as other sections joined in.

"Sonny! Sonny! Sonny!"

Soon it was deafening. Jerry Rice, who had his helmet off on the sidelines, looked at me and winked. Later in the dressing room he told me he was nervous to meet me because he had watched me on *All My Children*. For me, someone who as a little kid had watched the games and idolized the players, that was just the best moment.

While that evening and other projects made it an interesting interlude away from *General Hospital*, after a year I couldn't justify ignoring the standing offer to return. Finances always came into play, and it was different now that I had a family depending on me; I felt that protective instinct every time I looked at Paula and Cailey. Paula was supportive of whatever I wanted to do but also was quietly nervous about me being freelance again.

Around this time, Paula also decided she wanted to formally become my manager. I had always, of course, listened to her input on scripts, and she gave me advice on projects and my performance, but she wanted to take control where she thought agents hadn't before. She had gotten the bug for managing early on, but it wasn't until after Cailey was born that her confidence blossomed. So Paula formally took the reins as manager and has guided my career ever since.

I think Steve Burton says it best: "Paula's the wizard behind the curtain."

When Sonny and I both returned to Port Charles in 1999, his reappearance a little over a year after having been absent was orchestrated with quite a flair, revealing a depressed Sonny, who had been hiding out on his island away from everyone . . . until Jason figured it out, flew to get Sonny, and brought him home. And the fans went wild—their favorite mobster was back.

This time around, Donna was my makeup artist. Donna was tough, straightforward, and would tell it like it was no matter who you were. She was the peacemaker and could always keep situations from escalating. Everyone respected her honesty and came to her for advice. She knew about my bipolar, but she also wouldn't let me get away with any crap. If something bothered me and I was angry, Donna many times would help me see another side and I'd let it go. If I didn't agree with Paula about something and wanted to argue my point, nine times out of ten Donna would listen and then echo exactly what Paula said. I often told Paula that Donna was my Paula at work.

She also knew all the gossip and we talked every day about who was coming and going, the ratings, and life in general. We connected on so many levels, she was like a sister to me. I think Donna and I were real kindred spirits because we both had our guard up. I knew Donna hated hugs, and she knew I was just as uncomfortable being touchy-feely, so, like the little irritating brother, I hugged her all the time, just to bug her.

I saw a part of myself in Donna, the part that held people at arm's length, but one day when she revealed that her son, Nick, Jr., had struggled with anxiety over the years, I felt honored that she trusted me on that level. I tried to share some personal insight from my own struggles and we got closer. Although we mirrored each other to some degree, Donna knew how to communicate better than I did and she would push me to get better.

Carol Scott, a producer in her fifties, was another shining light on the set and a good friend. One day she came to work and was smiling from ear to ear; she had found her soul mate late in life and fallen in love.

A year later, when they got married and she was intensely happy, I was, too.

She was the person who I convinced to have Sonny show some vulnerability. One day I had a scene with Ron Hale that involved Mike and Sonny yelling and a lot of heightened emotion, which ended with Sonny near tears.

But later, when I watched it on tape, the moment wasn't there. They had cut away from me in that moment and I couldn't believe it, so I called the producers and went berserk.

"Who the hell cut it out?" I yelled.

"It was Carol's decision," one of them told me.

As always, Donna was there to give me some perspective, and I calmed down a little. Then I called Carol.

"Honey, why did you cut out the tears, what happened?" I asked.

"It would make Sonny look weak," Carol explained.

"No, it's the opposite. In that little moment you see his vulnerability," I told her.

She listened awhile and finally apologized, and after that they let Sonny express more emotion. That made me happy; finally, viewers could see the varying shades of Sonny.

One day I received a gift—one of those robots that lights up when you punch it. At the time, I hadn't boxed since high school and I realized I missed it. It's a gentleman's sport, I heard someone say once, and I think that's a good description. I decided to purchase a punching bag to work at home and get back into sparring and training at the gym.

I started out at Benny the Jet's gym and boxed there for years. Benny could still kick anybody's ass. They always played my favorite soul music, like James Brown, for me, and my trainer, Jeff Mulvin, helped me work out a lot of my anger in the ring (even though it once led to me accidentally dislocating his jaw). I also sparred a lot with another young trainer there, Majid Raees, who became a friend. He was always very spiritual, and the thing about Majid is he always tells you to do something in boxing or in life that annoys you, but he's always right. He would go on to become a sensei and train Kevin James and many other celebrities.

Boxing to me was a lot like acting. In a scene I don't want to know what's coming, a jab or a hook, because it's more interesting when things are unpredictable, saying lines faster or slower to switch it up. Same with boxing, where you have to react instinctively to whatever comes your way. My love of boxing eventually became part of Sonny's world. If you look closely in Sonny's house, you'll see a boxing picture hanging in Sonny's living room, commissioned by the show. Sonny also purchased a gym where he and everyone else in Port Charles worked out, a place named Voloninos, after our costume designer, Alice Volonino.

Off-screen, my own family continued to grow. At thirty-six, I became a father again when Cassidy Rose Benard was born on April 18, 1999. Just like her big sister, Cassidy was also born on a Sunday, but this time we preplanned the birth long before the due date came, since we had experienced the scare the first time with Cailey's Code Blue. I was not the only one in the room with Paula and Dr. Crane for the birth—Cailey, now almost five years old, and Heather, six, were also there. Thankfully this time there were no complications, and when Cassidy made her entrance into this world, again I cut the umbilical cord.

From the start, Cassidy was a quiet and gentle soul with the face of an angel and a great sense of humor. She was also the true cat lover in our family, which is fitting, since she seemed to have nine lives, always getting into dangerous scrapes and somehow coming out unscathed. Another music lover, when she was little she constantly hopped around singing, in her own little world, paying no attention to anyone or anything around her. One day she was hopping through the house and singing like she always did when suddenly we heard her sweet song stop abruptly, followed by screaming and loud bumping. We ran to see her in a pile at the bottom of the stairs, blood streaming down her face. She had tried hopping down the stairs and missed a step, but her tumble could have been far worse than the stitch or two she received.

Another time, workmen had the huge Sub-Zero refrigerator pulled away from the wall to open the plaster behind it in order to assess the damage caused by some pesky rats. At the end of the day, we told the girls not to touch the refrigerator, but after everyone was asleep little Cassidy came back downstairs and not only opened the fridge but climbed on a shelf to grab some food. As she did, the fridge started to tilt forward.

I woke up with a start as we heard a loud crash downstairs, and Paula and I bolted to see what had happened. We saw Cailey on the way down but no sign of Cassidy in her room, and as I ran downstairs in a panic, I called out for her but got no response. All I saw at first when I rounded the corner was the upended refrigerator, and my stomach tightened; I could only imagine little Cassidy pinned beneath it. As I sped across the kitchen to reach the refrigerator, a flood of relief hit me when I saw that on the other side of the huge, open door little Cassidy was squatting, frozen in horror. The door had miraculously swung open enough so that when the refrigerator fell, it stopped inches from crushing her—or trapping her inside it.

When she saw us, Cassidy jumped up, ran, and hid under the kitchen counter. She knew she had been told not to touch the refrigerator and thought she was in trouble, but when we saw what could have happened, all I wanted to do was grab my sweet girl and hang on to her for dear life, crying, grateful for the miracle.

Even after the refrigerator incident, there was also the marble incident, which was absolutely terrifying. That day, I saw Cassidy put a marble in her mouth, and as I said, "No! Please give that to me!" she ran instead like it was a game. As I started toward her, I suddenly saw that she was choking on it and I got behind her, attempting to do the Heimlich maneuver as I simultaneously called 911. The emergency operator told me *not* to do the Heimlich, but it was too late, I had already started. Now I was in a panic because I thought I had done more damage to my little girl, so I said a prayer, and as I did, the marble flew out of her mouth and she started to cry. So did I. Thank God, saved again, but Cassidy continued to have near-misses. I always say how grateful I am that her guardian angel was always working overtime.

My on-screen family also grew again, but it took a while.

During that time at work, the producers started putting Sonny with different girls, since Vanessa had left the show. Nothing was as special to the fans as the Brenda relationship—until lightning struck twice when they matched Sonny with Carly in a fiery one-night stand in 1999. Sarah Brown originated the character and was a phenomenon. Fans are super-protective; they act like they're my mother—they don't feel like anyone is good enough for Sonny except Brenda on the one hand and Carly on the other. Just as they couldn't get enough of Brenda and Sonny, now fans couldn't get enough of Carly and Sonny.

When the two moved in together, Sonny soon became a father figure to—and bonded with—her son, Michael. Although he wasn't the biological father, Sonny adopted Michael and raised him as his own, even though his and Carly's tempestuous relationship would result in on-again, off-again marriages to each other over the next decade.

When Sarah chose to leave the show several years later, Tamara Braun stepped into the role of Carly. The fans were so hooked on Sarah it seemed like an impossible task to win them over, but

Tamara and I worked hard and I truly think the vulnerability she brought to Carly turned it around.

Admittedly, there was a rough period during which I was difficult, because I absolutely hated the story line. Sonny shot Carly in the head by accident and she went into a coma. If that wasn't bad enough, while she was in the coma, she was in love with someone else, which meant that when she woke up, she didn't know Sonny. Not only did I hate the story line, but I made fun of it endlessly, to the point where Steve and I actually made Tamara cry. I'm ashamed that I was behaving no better than the bullies I had beaten up in school, but I didn't let up and complained to the producer, the writers, whoever was listening, including Donna, who also hated the story line.

"You're cutting Sonny's balls off!" I kept arguing.

They finally ended the story line, and I'm not sure if it's because it didn't work or that I was being such a pain in the ass. Even though she didn't like the dream story, Donna helped me see that I was being unfair to Tamara. I took full responsibility for my behavior and I apologized to Tamara and we resolved that bump in the road.

When Tamara later decided to leave the show, Jennifer Bransford came in, and I loved not knowing from one second to the next what she was going to do in a scene. But for whatever reason, the network decided to make a change. I fought for her and I even showed the president of the network a tape, but the network didn't support me on that, so Jennifer went on to better things.

And then Laura Wright came into Sonny's world. She was already popular on another soap when the producers decided to lure her to Port Charles, and since everyone knew I had fought for Jennifer, Laura probably felt like she was walking into an odd situation. She always tells me she tried to shake my hand and I wouldn't shake it, but the reason is that I had a cold. To this day, I'm not sure she believes me.

Laura knew how to steamroll it and she came in with two guns blazing, completely making Carly her own. Not only did her version become wildly popular at the beginning, but it has been incredibly successful for fifteen years now.

Doing scenes with Laura is like working with a force of nature, because she really fights for Carly, and I respect that. We've never gotten in a big argument, although I'm sure there are times when she wants to kill me. I also appreciate what a great scene partner she is when I'm having a dark period in my bipolar struggle. I always let her know if I'm going through something so she will be aware. She's such an incredible pro, she always knows how to handle it.

As the millennium approached, I continued to do films outside of *General Hospital*, including *Crystal Clear* as Steven, and then there was a changing of the guards at work. In 2000, Wendy and Shelley left the show and Jill Farren Phelps became the executive producer but Bob Guza was still head writer. He was brilliant at storytelling but they still always wrote Sonny as the bad guy and I used to argue all the time with Jill about that.

"How can I go to a knife fight with a toothpick?" I asked Jill over and over. "Sonny's always wrong; Jason's always the saint, saving the day. The whole town hates Sonny." I continued with a litany of examples. "Sonny was not a nice guy with Emily. Sonny shot his wife in the head, and the Quartermaines are against him. Michael got shot; it's Sonny's fault, because his enemies were after him. Even Luke, who's pretty much cool with whatever Sonny does, eventually was against Sonny. The list goes on."

Finally I asked if, just once, Sonny could be the hero. It wasn't that the character was unpopular, really; despite everything he did, he was wildly popular in the ratings. But I had to work my ass off constantly to be the charming mobster no matter what Sonny did. It was exhausting.

I used to always joke on set really loud so they'd hear it in the booth: "Everybody hates me. Who else hates me today?"

On days like that, Donna would cheer me up and try to get me not to take it so seriously.

Luckily, to balance out all that hate energy for my character all day at work, I had a lot of love at home and the year 2000 marked a milestone for me and my wife. It was our ten-year wedding anniversary and we had so much to be grateful for, including two healthy children. But in spite of all that, I knew Paula was sad because her wedding and engagement rings had been stolen one day that year. She was not only sentimental about the rings, but it brought back memories of her backyard wedding, reminding her that she never got to have her fairy tale day or wear the beautiful custom-made Cinderella dress still hanging in a zippered bag at the back of the closet.

And that's when I hatched a brilliant plan—I was going to throw Paula a surprise wedding. What could be better than that?

In the course of my planning, Paula, who usually made all the arrangements so our world ran smoothly, had seen a receipt for plane tickets for my parents to come visit, so she knew something was up, but figured it was birthday-related. She waited with anticipation, never letting on that she knew her in-laws were coming.

Since our ten-year anniversary had just come and gone, I figured I was in the clear as far as surprising her. She did finally ask me about the tickets, so I quickly came up with a crazy story explaining that for her birthday I was taking her to our friend Ricky

Martin's island because he was going to let us stay there for a get-away and I knew she wouldn't leave town without the kids, as she never left them alone overnight with anyone. I told her the island was large and my parents would stay with the kids on one side, while we stayed on the other. Paula thought it was plausible because she knew Ricky was a friend I'd met when he was playing Miguel Morez on *General Hospital*. He was by then at the height of success as a musician, so of course it seemed possible that he could own an island.

Paula was so touched that I had put together this surprise get-away she bought the entire lie. I told her I wanted to spend the night alone with her before leaving for the island, and took her to a hotel where we spent a romantic evening away, while my parents watched the kids. It was a rare occurrence for us to have an entire night to ourselves, a real luxury, since small kids were always running around and Paula always had a full plate of plans for them.

The next morning, I rolled out of the hotel bed and dropped to one knee.

Paula looked at me, asking, "What are you doing?"

"Marry me." I smiled, showing her a beautiful new diamond ring and matching band.

Paula admired the sparkling diamonds and put the rings on her finger, thrilled. Now it made sense to her. The rings were the surprise and my parents had flown in to celebrate our anniversary, she rationalized. "Honey, they're beautiful, thank you," she said, smiling.

"I'm serious, marry me," I said again. "You never got to have your Cinderella wedding, so let's do it."

"Yes, of course, baby, okay, let's plan it." She kissed me, playing along. "When would you like to?"

"Already done." I beamed. "We're getting married today."

"You're always such a joker." Paula laughed, but my face was not joking and the color drained from hers. "Today?" she continued in disbelief, before blurting out, "But I don't have a dress!"

"Also handled." I smiled proudly and presented Paula with a garment bag. She smiled politely, afraid to open it.

"Honey, you picked out a dress for me?"

"Better than that," I said, and with a flourish I unzipped the bag. Inside was the Cinderella ball-gown-style dress that had been in the closet for years, and when she saw it Paula burst into tears.

"Those are happy tears, right?" I asked, not understanding.

She could only shake her head no.

"But this is the dress you never got to wear," I said, puzzled.

It took her a moment to answer. Forget that it was a decade ago and styles were different, she had also had two children since then. But there was more.

"Honey, it was never finished!" she wailed, showing me the seams, which were held together with pins.

Paula frantically dialed her friend Julie, and they started calling around trying to find someone, anyone, who could help. It was too late to get another wedding gown, so they had to find a seamstress at the last minute who could do the next best thing: sew Paula into the gown on the spot.

I'm a guy; I figured, *Whew, problem solved!* I told her I had to leave to take care of the remaining details. This didn't exactly soothe Paula's misgivings—left to my own devices, what else had I done? I assured Paula a limo was on the way and left her half sewn, half pinned into her gown, waiting in the hotel lobby with a cell phone.

Paula felt like she waited an eternity. Then she waited some more. Julie called her, asking where she was, and Paula answered that she was still standing in the hotel lobby with every stranger there staring at her in her wedding dress. Clearly the limo I had "taken care of" never showed, and although Julie was helping with the rest of the wedding arrangements she got in her car and sped back to the hotel to pick up Paula. When she arrived, Paula stuffed herself and her dress as best she could into the small minivan, the reams of fabric enveloping them both, and at my request, Julie blindfolded Paula so she wouldn't know where she was going. Sitting in the van smothered in tulle, blindfolded, sweating, her hair and makeup hastily done herself, was not quite the fantasy wedding Paula had always dreamed about.

When the van finally stopped, Julie helped unstuff Paula from the vehicle and removed the blindfold. There, spread before Paula, in the back expanse of our Hollywood Hills home, was a truly storybook setting: against the beautiful blue sky, large arches framed the horizon, an explosion of various flowers—one of her favorite things—cascaded and spilled over everything.

Her relationship with her mother continued to be painful, and none of her family was there, but so many other people who adored Paula had been able to make it. There was my family, and our close friends, including Manny, Carol, and the rest of my *General Hospital* family. You could feel all the love in the room. Cailey, who was six years old, and Cassidy, who was two, appeared like two little angels in beautiful chiffon dresses, floating along with baskets of rose petals to scatter down the aisle.

I remember vividly that before Paula arrived the clouds were angry and black and threatening a torrent. But then Paula stepped out, with my father taking her arm, poised to walk her down the aisle for a second time, and the clouds parted. Suddenly four fighter planes came out of nowhere as her favorite Andrea Bocelli song played over the outside speakers. Guests assumed I had hired the jets for the ceremony and I just let that ride. Everyone was beaming as they stood watching her and she smiled back at them as she passed, walking toward me, stunning even in a dress from another decade—like a true fairy princess.

The entire setting and party were designed by Tolan Clark Florence, who is now married to chef Tyler Florence but at the time was the girlfriend of my *General Hospital* then–cast mate Billy Warlock who played A. J. Quartermaine, the real father of Sonny's son, Michael, and an archnemesis. I could have never pulled it off without her help and am forever grateful. Fitting for our nontraditional love story and wedding, I had my friend Jim Warren, a freelance photographer, take natural photos in the moment.

It wasn't exactly what Paula had planned all those years ago, but it was still a perfect day. We renewed our vows under a crystal-blue sky, celebrating a love story that had started during a troublesome period in both our lives, a love story that remained strong after all we had been through together. She told me later that the gesture meant more to her than anything.

With the wedding, and really everything else I did, my goal was to show Paula that our family was the number-one most important thing to me. Much like Sonny, I would do anything to protect my kids. Unlike Sonny, dangerous people weren't after my wife and family . . . yet.

Unfortunately, not long after our second wedding ceremony was when my fame began to negatively affect my children. It was more than excitable fans, and started to feel genuinely scary, when I began getting a lot of phone calls at work from a woman claiming to be Paula. Then one day an African American woman showed up at the Prospect Studios saying her name was Paula Benard. When the guards turned her away, I thought that was the end of it.

But then letters starting coming to our North Knoll house, and the woman wrote that she was coming from Cleveland to get her kids, implying that she thought our kids were hers. We didn't know how she had gotten our address and it wasn't until we noticed charges on Paula's credit cards for computers my wife had not purchased that we realized this woman had stolen Paula's credit card information and identity.

Worried about the vulnerability of the kids, we had security cameras installed everywhere along with a very high gate, with a keypad to enter and exit. We also spent a lot of money buying a German shepherd from Germany to police the house, but it turned out Glory was afraid of her own shadow. Paula was so terrified she even bought a gun.

We found out where my wife's impersonator was when we got a hospital bill in Paula's name, but even then the police still wouldn't do anything. Paula couldn't believe there was no recourse, she wouldn't accept that we had to live in fear every moment, or wonder if our kids were going to be accosted, so she kept pursuing a solution. Finally a detective Paula kept calling agreed to go to the hospital and talk to this woman.

When he arrived, she seemed perfectly normal. *General Hospital* was playing on the television and she was watching. And then she pointed at the TV where one of my scenes was playing. "That's my husband," she said.

When the detective asked, "What's your name?" she answered, "Paula Benard," without a hint of hesitation. He immediately called us and told us we had a real problem, explaining that getting a restraining order wasn't just hard, it was highly unlikely.

Paula wasn't deterred, and we hired a lawyer, filed the papers, and went to court. The detective was so concerned about the woman that he testified for us and told the court about his visit to the hospital and the woman's total delusion.

As we waited nervously for the outcome, our lawyer was surprised when the ruling favored us and we were granted a restraining order. Our lawyer told us if it hadn't been for that detective, it would probably have gone the other way. The woman was kept in an institution for over a decade that we were aware of, and sent me letters for years before we lost track of her.

The sad fact is, the woman suffered from mental illness and, like so many others, had fallen through the cracks in the system. She wanted to represent herself at the trial but wasn't allowed to because she was declared incompetent. I'm grateful every single day I had Paula in my corner to make sure that never happened to me. But clearly more work needs to be done in the community and laws need to change to help those who don't have a support system or can't help themselves.

While my focus was still on my family, this experience shook me to my core, and made me consider what I could do with my personal story, and my fame, to create a difference.

I knew I needed to be one of those voices for awareness and change.

CHAPTER ELEVEN

Beautiful Boy

As I learned after my stint in the mental institution, depression and bipolar disease are caused by a chemical imbalance in the brain. More than twelve million people in the United States and sixty million worldwide battle these disorders, and there is no cure. It is a lifelong commitment to manage the symptoms with the proper medication. It isn't just being "blue"—believe me, if you could just exercise and get the endorphins up, everyone who was afflicted would do it.

Diagnosing disorders can take a while, and accepting the diagnosis can take even longer. Pinpointing what combination of medication will help and the correct dosage is a crapshoot and can be frustrating.

If I'd only had this knowledge when I was young, maybe I wouldn't have had several breakdowns. I wanted others to know there were answers, and I wanted to push back against the stigma that prevents people from admitting they need help.

Until that point, I had hidden my illness from public view. I had been made to feel ashamed of it and was warned early on in the business not to expect people to understand. I was fearful that I wouldn't work if I disclosed my condition, so I had kept the secret. But after all these years, I was tired of that burden, and the recent scare my family had been dealt made it feel obvious I needed to act. I didn't want to continue silently carrying around the reality of who I was, and I didn't think others suffering from the disease should have to, either.

Even though it was scary, in 2000 I decided to do an interview in an obscure soap magazine that is no longer in print, discussing my condition. The response was overwhelming, and among the many thousands of people who sent letters about their own experiences, one in particular really impacted me. A kid wrote me a letter telling me his brother had shot himself in the head and he was finally able to deal with his brother's suicide after I talked about bipolar and where the depths of depression can take you. So many times family members and friends feel as if they have failed if they can't save you, and although their support is very important, the disease and the toll it takes are no one's fault.

Because of that letter, and the huge response to the article, I knew it was time to do more, so I decided to start working with mental health organizations and became the spokesman for the Depression and Bipolar Support Alliance (DBSA; formerly the National Depressive and Manic-Depressive Association). DBSA is the leading peer-directed national nonprofit organization providing support groups for people with depression or bipolar disorder as well as their friends and family, answering thousands of calls per month while distributing twenty-thousand educational materials free of charge. Their combined websites receive over twenty-one million hits and their online and face-to-face support groups have helped their members' hospitalization episodes decrease by almost half. Their programs prove that the power of people banding together is truly undeniable.

That year, I was chosen to give the closing address at the annual conference in Boston. I had talked to individuals one-on-one, but this was the first time I was stepping before an audience to tell my story. I had been in front of hundreds of fans, but this was different—this time there were five hundred psychiatrists in row after row, waiting to hear what I had to say. I was not disappearing inside a character; it was just me, emotionally naked in front of all those strangers, and it was a little terrifying, and at the same time amazing, to relate my story that day.

At the podium a clock in front of me was set for thirty minutes and that clock was a huge pressure—I felt like it was glaring at me, daring me to defy it. What if I couldn't speak eloquently or long enough in front of these smart, important people? Somehow I managed, and once I finished telling my story I heard applause, and it kept going for a while with a standing ovation that was humbling. Although it had been difficult it was one of the most fulfilling experiences I have ever had.

Another amazing mental health nonprofit I got involved with was the National Alliance on Mental Illness. NAMI is the largest organization in the nation dedicated to improving quality of life for those who suffer from mental illness. In 2001, I received the Lionel Aldridge Award for courage, leadership, and service to others with mental illness from NAMI, an award named after Lionel Aldridge, who was a former defensive end for the Green Bay Packers and won three world championships, including two Super Bowls but struggled for years with schizophrenia and homelessness.

Carrie Fisher, who dealt with mental health issues and was

an advocate like me, was also there, and Sally Field and Samuel Jackson were acknowledged that night for playing characters with mental illness. The ceremony was very special because it was the first big public event where I was honored for speaking out about my bipolar, and the work with NAMI has continued for twenty-plus years, helping bring awareness in any way they ask, from special events to speaking engagements and national campaigns including #CureStigma and #WhyCare.

Although the mental health work and my career took up the majority of my time, I was lucky to have the support of family and friends as I got more involved in activism. I was still in touch with my friend Manny, although it had been years since I talked to my old friend from home, Jeff.

So it came as a big surprise one day in January 2002 when Manny called—to talk about Jeff. He said he was living with Jeff, and that we should talk. God bless Manny, always the peacemaker.

I agreed. It had been so long and it was such a stupid fight.

Jeff got on the phone. As soon as he said, "Hey, man," it was like no time had passed, like we had never stopped talking. We stayed on the phone for an hour, laughing, and making fun of Manny, just like old times. When I got off the phone, I was happy we had reconnected.

But an hour later I got a call from Manny that would break my heart.

Manny told me that when Jeff hung up with me he was fine, but a few minutes later Manny heard him fall down the stairs. When he ran to help him Jeff was unconscious, so Manny called 911 and held him in his arms until the paramedics arrived. Jeff was in a coma and Manny was at the hospital waiting for the doctors to figure out what had happened. It turns out Jeff had meningitis and a few days later he succumbed to it without ever waking up from the coma. I didn't really get to say goodbye to him, but when Manny called me to tell me Jeff was gone, I'll always remember his take.

"Man, it looks like he needed to talk to you before he died," Manny said.

Jeff was only thirty-seven.

I had never before lost a close friend to death. You go through your life thinking everyone will always be around, that you're invincible, until suddenly a life ends and it's a loud, loud silence.

I wish I had made up with him before it was too late.

I wish I hadn't wasted all that time because of some argument that meant nothing in the grand scheme of things.

The point is, life is very, very short and you need to value the people in it. Beyond becoming aware I needed to use my platform to help others with depression and bipolar, this was by far the biggest lesson I learned during this time in my life.

Even though Jeff's death haunted me, I appeared not long after at the Didi Hirsch Mental Health Erasing the Stigma Awards ceremony. Didi Hirsch Mental Health Services is another wonderful organization I'm proud to support because it is the home of the first suicide prevention center in the nation for people contemplating suicide. It provides training and research and raises money that provides mental health services and substance abuse services in Los Angeles County. The Erasing the Stigma program meant so much to me and it was an honor to be acknowledged with the award because I know all too well what the stigma surrounding mental health can pressure a person to do.

The reception and luncheon took place at the Regent Beverly Wilshire in Beverly Hills, and again I was honored alongside

Carrie Fisher. Paula and I had been good friends with Carrie's brother Todd's wife, Catherine Hickland, since *All My Children*; at the time she was married to a costar. When we later attended Carrie's memorial it hit so close to home about what her struggles had been. Carrie was gone too soon and I hope she's at peace.

Rod Steiger was also awarded that day, and afterward the talented and wonderful Annette Bening presented an award to me. "Maurice plays a 'macho guy' on *General Hospital*, and macho guys—especially Latinos—don't go for help," Annette began, as people started applauding.

She was right. I was one of the first Latinos and actors to publicly discuss my bipolar disorder because I know how hard it is to come forward. It's hard enough, but very hard for guys, and then even harder culturally for Latino men. But the statistics can't be ignored and people need to learn to talk about it, accept it, and manage their disease, no matter what it is, no matter what sex they are or what their cultural confines. Depression and bipolar disorder are equal opportunity diseases and account for ninety percent of all suicides. Those numbers are staggering and so it means a lot to me every time I get one of these awards, because it's about something much bigger than me. I'm grateful I am healthy and alive and kicking and can try to help others deal with this terrible disease.

While I was spending time outside the show in the trenches of the mental health advocacy world, there was also a surprise return to Port Charles that enraptured fans and was another one of my all-time favorite stories and, in particular, favorite scenes.

Sonny and the rest of Port Charles assumed Brenda was dead from a car crash several years prior, and in this scene Sonny walks in the rain to St. Timothy's Church while "Amazing Grace" is playing and goes inside. While he's there, the doors open and suddenly

Brenda is standing before him, smiling. He's stunned, in shock, exuberant, but of course there's always something in the way of those two characters, and Sonny is shot by a character played by A Martinez. As he's dying in Brenda's arms, he asks Jason to promise to take care of her. It was well written, beautifully directed and shot, and so deeply emotional.

Sonny, of course, did not die but faked his own death to lure his enemy, Luis Alcazar, who had been holding Brenda prisoner, into the open. Sonny had also just had another child, his first girl, Kristina, with Alexis, his lawyer, played by the wonderful Nancy Lee Grahn. Sonny then went through a stint in jail and suffered extreme claustrophobia, and I had amazing scenes with Nancy in which the writers had crafted wonderful material for us with beautiful monologues helping Sonny deal with the debilitating fear of closed spaces due to his abuse as a child. Again the scenes were close to home for me and I had to go to some dark places to access those feelings, but I did it and managed to get through them.

Sonny also confronted his demons and confessed his sins to a priest in hopes of getting some understanding from God for the crimes he had committed as a mobster. It's a rich dynamic and always interesting to play those shades of Sonny's struggle between doing bad things and at the same time seeking absolution. It's also interesting to play Sonny the more the character changes, and I believe he changed the more people he had to love because the stakes in his world were different, and higher, with family and loved ones to worry about.

In May 2003, at the age of forty, I was nominated for another Emmy Award. Steve had started calling me the male Susan Lucci because I was always nominated and never won. Even though I acted like it didn't bother me, it did. The first few times I was nominated it meant too much to me and I was sure I'd win. I attended the ceremonies and waited, anxious, in the audience, and when someone else's name turned out to be in that envelope my heart sank. I had to decide not to let things I can't control *control me*. I have played the role of Sonny for almost half of my life, but I am not defined by it.

Even though the buzz was strong and many people were convinced I would win, I wasn't so sure, because in addition to lead actors from competing shows, I was up against the master himself, Tony Geary, from my own show. The day of the awards, a limo picked me up and my parents and Paula and our little girls attended with me. Paula looked beautiful as always in a gorgeous black dress, and Cailey and Cassidy were in adorable dresses with the crowning touch—a tiny tiara on Cassidy's little locks. Most of the show, Cassidy sat in Paula's lap, and fell asleep before my category was even announced, but Cailey was transfixed by all the beautiful gowns and felt like such a grown-up staying up late at the adult function.

As Erika Slezak, a veteran of *One Life to Live*, read all the actors' names who were nominated for Best Actor, and as the clips of scenes were played on the huge screen, Paula squeezed my hand. After the applause died, Erika opened the envelope.

"The winner is Maurice Benard!"

The auditorium, filled to the rafters with fans and my peers surrounding me, exploded in a deafening roar. Stunned, and with a racing heart, I made my way to the stage and pulled out my notes. I began by telling the fans they were the best, because they are, and I then gave a shout-out to Tony, who was smiling and clapping for me offstage.

"We wouldn't be here if it wasn't for you," I said, nodding

to him, and went on to thank the network, my agents, and the producers. When I got to the writers I was on fire. "To the writers, Bob and Chuck, thanks for getting this character. Elizabeth Korte, thanks for writing such brilliant words. And all the writers, if it ain't on the page it ain't on the stage!"

More applause erupted in the audience and I could barely hear myself talk. "To the director and crews, I love you guys," I said, as I choked back tears. My voice wavered slightly, because I was looking out at my wife and girls in the audience and thinking about them as well as my parents, who were somewhere in the crowd. The fans and most of the people in the auditorium had no idea what I had gone through with my parents, Paula, doctors, hospitals, therapists, and medication to get to this point, on this stage, holding this shiny award. When the orchestra started playing music to get me off the stage, I waved them off, ignoring the cue.

"To my mother and father, to Cailey and Cassidy, to my wife who was sent from above, I love you." I barely got the words out; partly because I thought my heart would burst, but partly because I was still struggling with that emotional aloofness that makes it so hard to say those things out loud to the people I'm closest to in the world. In a strange way the camera helped, like having to read lines in a scene.

Paula wiped her own tears as she listened, and the entire place rose to their feet for a standing ovation. It was one of the best moments of my life and I flashed a peace sign, holding my Emmy above my head. I had dreamed about this from the day I'd decided to act, and Paula had dreamed about it, too, never giving up on me and always helping me to get there. My parents had never given up on me, either, and my mom was crying and my dad clapped louder than anyone else there, proud of his son.

My mom loved this outfit, I hated it.

My big bro, H.J.—or Humbug—
always had my back. I love him.
And how about those dimples?

That towering, scary man
was also a loving father that
happened to be my hero.

My good-looking parents all dressed up with their boys. Goodbye, 1970s.

College Park High School, Class of 1981. It was a miracle I graduated. But man, did we celebrate.

And the love story begins . . .

The "Most Watchable Man" meets the most beautiful girl in the world.

The day I asked my wife to marry me

August 11, 1990—the day I married my wife at my parents' house. Here we are with my brother, H.J.

Photo courtesy of Jim Warren

The day I surprised my wife with the wedding she never got. The sky was black, and I was so nervous the wedding would be ruined, but the moment she walked down the aisle, the clouds parted and a clear beautiful sky appeared.
Photo courtesy of Jim Warren

It took me ten years to make it up to my wife and have her dream wedding. Our daughters made it just perfect.

Paula and I had our first wedding in my parents' backyard, and this one—our second—was in our own backyard. It was a dream to have my whole family be a part of my celebration of love for my wife.

My kids are my whole world

Photo courtesy of Jim Warren

Cassidy *Photo courtesy of Jim Warren*

Above: Cailey *Bottom:* Heather

Joshua

The love my kids have for Paula melts my heart.
Photo courtesy of Jim Warren

We adopted Heather when she was thirteen, but she was always a part of our lives.

Above: Cassidy

Left: Girls rule our house. *Photo courtesy of Soaps in Depth*

Above: My boy, Joshua *Right:* Oprah's *Where Are They Now? Photo courtesy of Jim Warren*

Left: Sharing my second shocking Emmy win with my lovely Cassidy

Bottom: Sharing my first Emmy win with three-year-old Cassidy

Right: Greatest night ever! My dad was so happy.

Below: My wife is always by my side.

All photos courtesy of Jim Warren

General Hospital, Family Affair

Steve Burton is a brother to me, he has always had my back. And he's an incredible actor. *Photo courtesy of Jim Warren*

The dream team

Tony Geary is my dear friend and a true legend. *Photo courtesy of Jim Warren*

My kids grew up at *General Hospital*. From left to right: Jason Thompson, Heather Benard, Jonathan Jackson, Cailey Benard, Nathan Parsons, Drew Garrett. *Photo courtesy of Jim Warren*

General Hospital's Christmas party. The "Boss" with Old and Young Sonny.

Sonny and Jason may hate Jax, but we are great "mates" outside of work.

Kin Shriner, my close friend, who's always making me laugh

This is how I feel every time I work with Max Gail.

My new friend, Stephen A. Smith, Mr. Jack-of-All-Trades, star of ESPN, now starring on *General Hospital* as Brick. Matt Cohen is a genuine soul.

All photos courtesy of Jim Warren

Left: Dominic Zamprogna is not only a great actor but a great friend. *Photo courtesy of Jim Warren*

Bottom: Chad Duell, Bryan Craig, and Joshua. I gave Chad a hard time initially but we then became close friends. What Bryan did with the bipolar story line was second to none. *Photo courtesy of Melissa Heck*

Lexi Ainsworth is very sweet but fierce!

Above: Eden McCoy is so pleasant to be around. *Photo courtesy of Jim Warren*

Left: These twins steal my heart. *Photo courtesy of Jim Warren*

These women are all so talented and it's been a pleasure to work with them. Talk about Girl Power!

Right: Laura Wright
Photo courtesy of Soaps in Depth

Victoria Gotti

Genie Francis

Vanessa Marcil
Photo courtesy of Soaps in Depth

Donna Messina, December 6, 2018

My need to express myself outside of *General Hospital*. Thank you, Frank Valentini. Joshua and I at the screening for my first horror film. *Photo courtesy of Jim Warren*

One of my toughest roles to date, playing John Gotti *Photo courtesy of Jim Warren*

My proud mom and dad *Photo courtesy of Jim Warren*

The Ghost and the Whale. Proudly produced by my wife, Paula. *Photo courtesy of Jim Warren*

The Ghost and the Whale

My dad is one of the funniest men I know. I love having him on stage with me, except when he steals the show from me and doesn't want to leave the stage.

Speaking out on mental health has and always will be my biggest passion in life. It's the reason for this book. I hope to see you all on the road when I begin my *State of Mind* tour.

Embrace Real Artists, Talent Agency. Frank Cammarata, me, Joshua.

All photos courtesy of Jim Warren

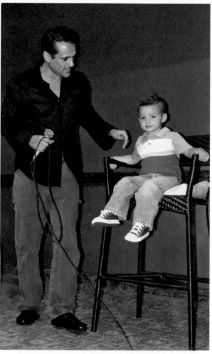

My boy, Joshua, has been on stage with me since he was two years old. Talk about a natural talent.

My boy, Joshua
Photo courtesy of Jonathan Antin

Cain. Miss you, bud.

Buddy the Goat

Heather and Phil Anderson
Married June 29, 2019
SERGEANT, UNITED STATES
MARINE CORPS
*Photo courtesy of Lukas
VanDyke*

*My girls
all found real
heroes*

Cailey and Carlos Avila
Soon to be married
June 6, 2020
FIREFIGHTER
Photo courtesy of Jim Warren

Cassidy Rose Benard and
Anthony Cammarata
UNITED STATES AIR FORCE
Photo courtesy of Jim Warren

I was proud of, and pleased for, Vanessa, too, when she also won an Emmy that night and we all celebrated together at the after-party. The windows of the venue were covered so no one could see in, and Mom, Dad, Paula, and the kids were all dancing and having so much fun that we partied until six a.m. Best night of my life.

Aside from the Emmys, May also marks mental health awareness month. I had gotten involved in Mental Health America (MHA; formerly the National Mental Health Association of America) to become the spokesperson that year for the Do You Know It Campaign, which played during that month to promote awareness about mental health issues. MHA is the nation's leading community-based nonprofit dedicated to addressing the needs of those living with mental illness, including prevention services, intervention for those at risk, integrated care, service, and support with recovery as the goal. It promotes education, research, services, and advocacy, collaborating with affiliates and supporters to advance policy recommendations and protect the rights of individuals. Countless times moms had told me their children were suicidal, or individuals wrote me asking for advice because they were so depressed, so as I expanded the number of programs that I gave my time to, it helped me to know that I was helping others.

The high from the Emmys and all the life work I was accomplishing was replaced in 2004 with news that came as a terrible blow. My dear friend Carol had cancer. I heard the c-word and my dark thoughts of course took me down a very dark road, imagining the worst. Carol, however, was positive and she was sure she was going to beat it, so she started treatment and we all said prayers. Donna did her best to distract me at work and keep us all upbeat about Carol's prognosis.

We got some good news to cling on to when we found out Paula was pregnant. I have to admit I secretly hoped for a boy, but when we were told we were having another girl and I realized I would be the *only* man in a house surrounded by females, I figured that could be fun. Once it got out publicly that we were having a girl, the fans thought it was great that I was going to be a father to three girls, too.

As we continued to say prayers for Carol, Paula prepped the house and filled the nursery drawers with clothes for a baby girl, but about six months into her pregnancy we got a surprise. One day at Paula's routine obstetrician visit, Dr. Crane took a look at the sonogram and then studied it more closely. Paula was afraid something was wrong, but Dr. Crane just smiled and showed Paula that the little person growing inside her was definitely *not* a little girl.

When she called to tell me, I wouldn't take her seriously; I thought it was a joke and told her it wasn't funny. I explained that I was really excited about having all girls and defended myself, reiterating that I was really okay with it. It took Paula several moments to convince me that she was serious, and when it finally dawned on me that I was having a son I was speechless. I was truly exhilarated and terrified at the same time. It would be amazing to have a father-son bond; naturally it's different than the bond a father has with his daughter.

But at the same time, I wondered, *What if he's just like me?* and I had to fight my dark thoughts.

That year the Los Angeles City Council acknowledged me with an award for contributing to raising awareness of mental health issues. Antonio Ramon Villaraigosa, who would be elected mayor the next year, gave me the award. Mr. Villaraigosa told me his friends and family had told him that he looks like me and we had a laugh about maybe being related. After the ceremony, someone in Mr. Villaraigosa's office came over and thanked me for helping to save their son's life. *That's* what this is all about.

As I waited for my son to arrive, I had a huge life realization. Maybe it was brought about by being a father and worrying about my own children and how they would grow up, what challenges they would face. Maybe it was also having watched Carol valiantly fight for more time on this earth for so many months. Either way, I knew time was precious and I didn't want to waste any of it.

I had to go public in a big way with my bipolar story.

In November 2004, I agreed to appear on *Oprah* to share my struggle with the disease.

Being on *Oprah* is somewhat like auditioning for a movie—there are multiple phone conversations before a representative from the show then comes in person for a pre-interview session. That all happens before you ever sit with the wonderful Oprah herself. Winning an Emmy had been a dream of mine, and so was being on her show, but this was not exactly the way I had visualized it when I was starting out as a young actor. I had imagined how cool it would be to sit on Oprah's couch and chat with her about cool things. Now that I was perched next to Oprah in front of a live audience, knowing millions were also watching, one of the first questions was far more difficult to answer than I'd thought.

"Maurice, how did it feel to threaten to kill your wife?" Oprah asked me.

It was such a personal and unattractive memory and this was such a gigantic, famous public forum; it was hard to describe and relive that dark terrifying night I'd put Paula through hell when I was off my meds. Paula was eight months pregnant by this time, and although she didn't like attention, she went on the show with me because she knew how hard it was going to be for me. When Oprah asked me that, I turned and searched Paula's sweet face, and in her eyes I saw what I needed to see—I knew it would be okay. We were doing the right thing; we had to speak out to try and make a difference in the lives of so many who suffered silently, afraid to talk about a mental disorder most didn't understand. I was determined not to cry, but that was a hard interview.

Another big emotional moment came soon after, when Joshua James was born on December 5, 2004. As with both his sisters before him, Joshua's birth was induced on a Sunday. The day Joshua came into the world, my parents were there along with Cailey, Cassidy, Heather, and my friend Mfundo Morrison, *General Hospital* character Justus Ward, the grandson of Edward Quartermaine.

No matter how many times you go through it, it really is a miracle watching a new soul enter your life. It's magical, a gift from God. I was immediately full of awe that this little boy might look at me the way I had looked at my dad, wanting to be like him. It also worried me because I didn't want my relationship with him to be the same.

We set up his crib in our room because Joshua was born with severe asthma and spent a lot of time in the ER when he was little. It was painful to watch him struggle to breathe, and there were nights I was worried, thinking people could die from this.

Although Joshua pulled through, I found out that Carol wasn't faring as well. When she didn't show up to work in the spring, I asked Donna where she was, and she said Carol wasn't coming back because she only had a few months to live. It was strange to be so happy for the new child in our life while at the same time knowing that Carol was losing her battle with cancer.

On June 27, 2005, Carol left this earth. She was only fifty-six.

Donna and I talked about it a lot, and I leaned on her heavily. I felt bad that I hadn't been there for Carol the last few months, and that I hadn't seen her, but Donna told me Carol didn't want anyone to see her that way because she said it would be too hard to say goodbye. Carol's husband reiterated that when I spoke to him. It was just devastating that she'd only had a few years with her soul mate.

ABC hosted a beautiful memorial for Carol at the ABC Prospect Studios where Carol had spent so much of her life and imagination and energy on the show she loved so dearly. Everyone gathered on the soundstage and there were beautiful loving stories about Carol, as well as many tears.

There was a huge hole at work where Carol had been, and it was hard to get used to being on set without her. I found myself turning to say something to her so many times, and every time she wasn't there it broke my heart again. She was one in a million.

We continued to have our own close calls and scares with Joshua's severe asthma attacks. I felt so bad for Joshua because his asthma impacted everything. He didn't play sports, and wasn't on teams when he was small, like I was, because of his condition. That's probably why he didn't have the same interest in sports as me or in watching football games with me like I had with my dad as a kid.

I was struggling in other ways as I raised my son. When Joshua was little, he was a pain in the ass, like the universe was paying me back for all the trouble I'd gotten into as a kid. When he's like that, Paula always says, "Talk to your son."

One night when he was about seven, he wouldn't eat his dinner because he was on his phone; when I told him to eat, he ignored me. I was so angry I took his phone away from him and threw it, but he still wouldn't listen to me. I started toward him and he ran, so I began to chase him, racing after him all the way up the stairs before he locked himself in the bathroom with Cassidy. I started yelling through the door and pounding on it. I was so worked up I didn't know what to do. I was afraid I was capable of hurting him, given my upbringing, but fortunately my good friend Melissa Heck was over for dinner and calmed me down.

The older Joshua got, the more I wanted to break the chain of what I had dealt with as a child. I didn't want to be like that with my own kids; I didn't want to use physical violence and I didn't want to be emotionally aloof.

It would be easier for me to achieve the former.

With my daughters, it wasn't complicated because they were so well behaved, but Joshua's behavior could drive me up the wall. The thing is, you're operating out of fear when you use rough physical discipline, and you may achieve respect but you don't get something else that is really important—a closeness and a love and a joy that I can't even describe. I realized if I wanted to break the chain, I had to find an alternative way to communicate with my sensitive son.

I started talking to Joshua softly. I reined in my aggressive, angry reaction to his disobedience. And it worked.

Joshua was also always glued to video games, which worried me. One night there was a *20/20* segment on TV about being addicted to video games.

"Hey, Joshua, come watch this with me, it's pretty cool," I said.

After a minute or two of watching, he squirmed. "I don't

need this, Dad," he told me, but he paid attention and I think he understood what the program was saying. When it finished, he didn't go back to playing his games right away. He sat there with me and then finally said, "All my friends are online, playing the game with me."

"What about your other friends?" I asked. "Why don't you invite them over more?"

He hesitated a beat and then finally said quietly, "I don't have any other friends."

It broke my heart and I gently said, "Well, maybe these online strangers aren't the right friends."

But Joshua's school days had been much different than mine even though he was uninterested in studies like me. He had been homeschooled when he was younger and when we let him go to public school, he had a tough time. He didn't make friends, and, in fact, he finally admitted he was bullied. After that I decided to show him how to box in order to defend himself, and the first time he put on the gloves and hit me I could feel the solid lead in that kid's hands. By this time I had moved on to the Wild Card Gym and I'd take Joshua with me to train. We met Manny Pacquiao there, which was very cool, because I love watching him fight.

Once, when Joshua and I were sparring, he started wheezing. He always has the inhaler but it's still scary when it happens; however, Joshua doesn't let that stop him. He's good at whatever he tries, and if he's passionate about it, look out. When I started working with him, I knew he could be a pro, but Paula won't allow it.

School continued to be a problem, though, and when Joshua was in sixth grade, Paula got a call from the principal asking her to come to his office. When she got there, she found out the bullying had gotten worse and now involved several students. Paula was upset because she had decided to let him attend public school but the experience was ruined and Joshua couldn't even enjoy school or meet new friends because of the bullying.

That night, Joshua told me that he would fight the bullies, but Paula was not going to let that happen—that was not why Joshua was going to school. The look she gave me said it all. She did not want Joshua to repeat my formative school years, which were centered around winning altercations instead of getting an education. So we decided to continue Joshua's homeschooling and enrolled him in a more creative online school where he soon started taking more of an interest in his studies.

While I was experiencing the father/son dynamic in my own world, once again my personal life paralleled Sonny's, because Sonny was now a father to *his* first biological son, Morgan. Sonny had delivered the baby himself, and it quickly became one of my most relatable story lines.

Around this time, the *General Hospital* producers approached me with an idea that really could help people—they wanted to add bipolar disorder to Sonny's traits. I had thought about it prior to that, but mostly, up to that point, I had not overtly asked to make bipolar an actual diagnosis for Sonny. I had just on my own started putting little hidden layers of depression into Sonny's dark times. But now there was an opportunity to actually shine a light on it, give a name to it, and draw international attention to bipolar and depression on a daily stage.

At the time, Sonny had begun a relationship with Jason's sister, Emily Quartermaine, played by the talented Natalia Livingston, who was a joy to work with. She did an incredible job making Sonny's bipolar story resonate realistically and emotionally. Sonny's brother, Rick, played by the great Rick Hearst, exacerbated

Sonny's situation, pushing him over the edge, and all through July 2006 Sonny's mental health declined as he descended into a breakdown.

It was very realistic; Sonny resisted believing he had mental illness, and when Emily confronted him and told him he was probably bipolar he wouldn't accept that. When she convinced him to see a therapist he put it off, but finally when he did face a trained doctor, in those sessions Sonny was diagnosed with bipolar disorder. Then the real struggle began as he fought taking lithium, afraid he would be a medicated zombie. The writers did a fantastic job because it was honest and authentic; I related to every beat of his struggle. After all, I had lived it.

I taped a public service announcement that aired during this time talking about bipolar and directing viewers to look for signs, and numbers were given to call if they felt they or someone they knew might be afflicted. The response to the story was enormous, and again, all sorts of letters began flooding in from people who struggled themselves and identified with me, or people who were worried about a relative, or friends who wondered if their loved one needed help. I'll never forget one letter from a woman who thought her husband was bipolar, and after she got him to watch the show during that time he finally admitted he needed help. She told me it had saved their marriage—and his life. I was so proud that the powerful force of art of any kind could mean something bigger in the grand scope of things.

Although I felt the need to continue to bring awareness to bipolar, the melding of my personal and professional lives eventually took its toll. While Sonny was going through darkness and turmoil, I was on my meds, so I thought I was okay, I thought I was handling it, but the intensity of the story and the memories I had to access as a method actor to get to those dark places were pulling me down again. I just didn't realize how far down.

I had to fly to Pittsburgh for an appearance along with Ron Hale, and as we were boarding, some guys looked me up and down with a sneer.

"Fuck you guys," they yelled, taunting me.

I started getting stressed and I could feel the anger rising like my old high school brawling days with my buddies.

"You guys are fucking special," they continued to harass me.

Suddenly I couldn't control my rage. "Why don't we go outside and I'll tell you the whole story?" I said menacingly, preparing to grab one of the guys. It was as if I were on the playground, fists tight, unwilling to back down. Ron pulled me away before I could hurt the guy and made me take my seat. I managed to doze off; however, soon I began fighting an unseen demon in my sleep, talking out loud while tossing and turning and flailing my arms. Ron woke me and I had a full-blown anxiety attack, hyperventilating and unable to calm down. Mercifully, we finally got to Pittsburgh, but my panic attack on the plane had spooked me, because I had absolutely no control over it.

I got through the appearance okay and I took a Xanax before boarding the flight home, thinking that would take care of it, but the minute I boarded I could feel the anxiety rising and I couldn't sit in my seat. I felt like my entire insides were on fire, like I was burning from within and I needed to take my clothes off. Ron tried to talk me out of it, but I kept insisting I had to get off the plane and got more and more belligerent.

My behavior elevated the situation to high alert, and I'm sure my brown skin didn't help matters, nor did the post-9/11 panic about airline security. The flight attendants told the pilot, who called security, and they had to delay the takeoff and open the door to deboard me. The cops were waiting and escorted me off the plane and into the terminal, and once I was on solid ground I started to calm down. The cops were deadly serious and it took a lot of talking to get out of that situation, but God bless Ron, somehow he convinced them I was on a TV show and also bipolar and was no threat. A few months later when I received my fifth Emmy nomination, I didn't attend the ceremony because I was nervous about getting on a plane again. Once again, I knew I needed to do the work in therapy, but I would struggle with the aversion to planes for a while.

Meanwhile, in 2007, four parents in San Diego, California with children affected by bipolar disorder and the trauma that it causes for them and their families started a group called the California Bipolar Foundation in order to do something constructive to help. As the foundation rapidly grew, it became the International Bipolar Foundation (IBPF), with a scientific advisory board to improve understanding and treatment of bipolar disorder through research. It also promotes care and support resources for individuals and caregivers and works to erase stigmas through education. Their vision is to achieve wellness, dignity, and respect for people living with bipolar disorder. It is a wonderful organization and co-founder Muffy Walker worked with us coordinating many events, advocating tirelessly.

I was also honored that year by the Depression and Bipolar Support Alliance for raising awareness and fighting the stigma of mental health issues. But in 2007, I had the opportunity to go all the way to Washington, D.C., to raise awareness on the largest national scale of all when I was asked to testify before Congress. Even though the first bill attempting to address mental health parity coverage introduced by Republican Senator Pete Domenici and Democratic Senator Paul Wellstone (previously authored by Domenici and Republican Senator John Danforth in 1992) had passed in 1996, it was extremely limited and did not require insurance companies to offer mental health insurance. So, for the most part, insurance companies had been getting around paying for mental health costs ever since. Congress had also been bickering over different bills by different members of Congress trying to change that—and powerful special interest groups opposed made that change languish—for a decade. Even when George W. Bush created the New Freedom Commission on Mental Health and called for parity in 2001, it faced an uphill battle.

Since 2001, the wonderful mental health nonprofits I was involved in, NAMI and MHA, had been fighting the insurance companies and special interests who had succeeded in stalling numerous attempts to pass legislation in favor of coverage for mental illness.

I was happy to use my face and name to advocate for why people need this coverage. Everyone was pulling out all the stops to get the bill passed, and I wanted to do my part and speak at the hearings. I'm blessed in my life, but without insurance companies acknowledging mental illness medical bills, anyone can lose it all, and lose it fast.

The timing, however, turned out to be terrible. I was deep into another story line on the show involving Sonny having a manic episode, stopping his meds, and spiraling down. Of course, since I'm a method actor, I had been *living* Sonny's downward dive into darkness for weeks, and even though I thought I was successfully separating the two, sometimes Sonny's struggle took me further into my own. Donna noticed I was having trouble and was there for me, as always, trying to calm me and focus me and let me know things would be all right, but I was already going down that dark rabbit hole I had gone down before.

Once again I started hearing voices, just like I had years before during my first month on the show. I was also seeing things, including visions of my parents on set and in rooms when they were clearly not in town. Once, in the middle of the night, the voices in the room were so loud they woke me and I lay there in the darkness, my breath coming in short spurts, trying to tell myself no one was in the room but me and Paula, who was sound asleep beside me. But the voices kept whispering to me, saying dark things, and although I tried to shake them, they got louder and louder in my head, drowning out reality. I finally got up and went out on the balcony, trying to get air because I couldn't breathe, and I only started to calm down a little when I heard Paula call to me from inside.

"Babe, what's wrong?"

"I'm hearing the voices again."

Paula, as she always does, took control, canceling my flight to Washington, D.C., and apologizing to the congressional liaison, explaining that I was ill and wouldn't be able to speak before Congress the following day. She also called Jill, our executive producer, and bluntly told her I would not be shooting any more scenes about a breakdown and the current story line had to end immediately.

I was not off my meds this time, and that's what made it even scarier. This new nemesis that had reared its head was worse than the depression I had dealt with up to this point in my life. This new demon was even more crippling. It was extreme anxiety and it would come for me again.

I wouldn't fly anywhere for almost a decade.

I attempted once shortly after that because Paula had planned a family vacation to Puerto Rico. I was the last in line to board, but as I started up the ramp, the panic of anxiety gripped me with a chokehold, so I told Paula I had to get off the plane and she rallied the children and gathered our things, returning to the terminal. Never one to disappoint the kids, Paula rented a motor home and we drove across the country for an alternate vacation the kids enjoyed, but I still felt bad that I had ruined our original plan.

I related to Sonny more than ever, because Sonny's transgressions had started to put his family in danger and, similarly, I knew that every time I had a manic episode, my children and my wife were at risk. I had not had a breakdown or threatened any violence during one since I'd had kids, because I had been on my meds, but the possibility of a depression was always lurking.

So were the anxiety and panic attacks. My dad always asks me, "Which is worse? Depression or anxiety?" Although they're both poison, for me, I think it's anxiety. When you're depressed, it's terrible; you're down, you don't feel like doing anything, you feel heavy, but anxiety is worse, it's like an explosion waiting to happen. When you're having a good day or a good week or month, it feels like an angel is inside you, and then, suddenly, the demon comes back. The depression demon sits inside you and makes you feel heavier than you can imagine. The anxiety demon makes your thoughts go a hundred miles an hour and you can't sleep, which makes you freak out, which makes it worse.

Whenever I have a dark period, I just want to stay in bed. If I have to go to work, it's tough, because I have to show up in front of a camera. I'm lucky I have a supportive show and supportive cast-mates but if either the depression or anxiety hits over a weekend, or on a family vacation, I have often curled up and drawn the shades and stayed in the dark. It's not good to do that; it's better to keep moving, keep going through the motions, but there are times I gave in to just trying to disappear.

Whenever that happens, Paula always tells the kids, "Dad is sick," and they learned at a young age to leave me alone when I'm in that state. If they wanted to play or be loud, Paula just let them know I wasn't feeling great, and somehow they knew it wasn't the normal kind of sick like when they had a tummy ache. They understood, and I love them for accepting me even though it may not always have been fun for them.

In 2007, Oprah also wanted to do a follow-up interview, to check in and see how my mental health journey was going, but we had to tape the show at our home in Los Angeles because I still couldn't get on a plane. Oprah talked to me via satellite from Chicago and I told her it had been a rough patch. I apologized for not being there in person and explained that the last time I had tried to fly I had disappointed my family.

To this day, I still regret not being able to make that trip to Puerto Rico, for my family's sake, but especially for Joshua, who had never been on a plane and was so excited he had been anticipating it for weeks before I took that experience away from him.

How do you explain to a child something that makes no sense?

When anxiety grips me, I can't breathe. It's like being in a cage with a wild animal and I have no idea when I'm going to die because that beast is looking at me and I know it's going to devour me alive. It's just a matter of time.

Although my anxiety kept me from testifying before Congress, others did, and the continued efforts of mental health organizations pressuring for insurance companies to cover mental health finally paid off. Despite the many years the House and Senate had clashed over it, when Lehman Brothers declared bankruptcy and a financial meltdown ensued, the crisis created a new path forward. Democratic Representative Patrick Kennedy and Republican Representative Jim Ramstad used their previously stalled mental health parity bill H.R. 1424 and garnered votes to tie it to the bailout in the Emergency Economic Stabilization Act of 2008. An ill Senator Edward Kennedy helped gather support for the bill, and hours after it passed both houses of Congress, George W. Bush signed the bill into law to stabilize the banking industry—and legally constitute mental illness as a condition requiring coverage by insurance companies on par with medical illness.

It couldn't have been done without Senator Paul Wellstone, a Democrat, who had watched his family pay off overwhelming medical debt for twenty years after his older brother, Stephen, spent two years in a mental hospital in a catatonic state. Or Republican Senator Pete Domenici, who had a schizophrenic daughter and found it difficult to secure insurance coverage for her needs. Republican Senator John Danforth, Democratic Senator Edward Kennedy, and his son, Democratic Representative Patrick Kennedy, himself diagnosed as bipolar, all advocated for laws to change, as did Republican Senator Michael Enzi, Democratic House Speaker Nancy Pelosi, and Democratic Senate Majority Leader Harry Reid, whose personal connection to the issue was losing his father to suicide as a young boy. The point is, mental illness touches everyone, no matter your station in life and no matter your political preference. People on both sides of the aisle pushed for this law that can make the difference between a family losing their house to cover mental health care treatment bills or not. I wonder where that spirit in Washington has gone.

Although Senator Wellstone perished in a plane accident before seeing a parity law come to fruition, his legacy lives on in the statute Congress finally passed that makes it illegal to financially discriminate against those with mental health needs. I and I'm sure thousands of others are forever in his debt—and all the others who used their power for good. Our health care system is constantly under attack by special interest groups and forces trying to turn back the clock on many of these rights, which is why it's so important to support nonprofits and find ways to get involved.

We can't stop fighting for those rights because people need mental health insurance as much as they need insurance for the removal of a cancerous tumor. Both are dire circumstances, and if left unattended they can kill you . . . and far too often do.

CHAPTER TWELVE

Tears in Heaven

When I was growing up, my father always said, "Lo que pasara pasara," which means, "What will happen will happen." You can't fight the course of life, you can only accept that there will be both good and bad things that come your way. H.J. had grown up knowing that, but I had resisted, I was full of fight. I didn't understand why bad things had to happen, and often railed against the inevitability facing me.

I had already lost Jeff and Carol too young. In 2007, another friend, Ray, died at the age of fifty.

He was another person I didn't get to say goodbye to, another soul who died too young, and it was hard to believe one day he was there, and the next he wasn't. I kept thinking I would see him drive up to the house or hear that great laugh of his, but he left another very big, very loud silence behind in my world. Paula was also devastated, and neither of us could fight the tears at his funeral. I was reeling because the deaths of three people so close in my orbit put me in a dark place. I couldn't shake it. Paula had just the right medicine in mind—she decided I needed a dog.

Paula knew how healing animals can be for the spirit because they are the purest spirits of all. I had always wanted an Akita, so that's exactly what Paula found for me. When we picked the puppy up, I remember this little fluffy black-and-white face that looked like a tiny bear peeking out at me from his carrier, and that was it, I was his.

It took a year and a half for Cain to figure out I was the leader and to do what I said, but even after that he was still a handful. He attacked dogs all the time, and whenever I scolded him, he looked at me with big sorry eyes like it was something wild inside him he couldn't control. That's probably why I bonded with him—I knew all too well that wild uncontrollable part of me inside somewhere that can unleash itself at any time.

I took him everywhere with me and we went on long walks every day. He even came with me on *The View* one time in Los Angeles and they all loved him. Martin Lawrence wanted one like him and called to ask me where I got him. He was so stunning, people actually stopped in their cars to take pictures, and whenever I took him in the car with me, people also not only stopped and stared but gave me crazy looks. At first I didn't understand the freaked-out, scared expressions on their faces, but the mystery was finally solved one day when I glanced in the rearview. Cain always sat in the back with his head hanging out; however, it looked like a real bear was in the car, because the wind had blown all his hair back.

Cain had a beautiful soul. He knew I was hurting and he comforted me and knew when others needed comfort, too. One time I was walking with Cain and my mom and dad in L.A. and a homeless guy came up yelling crazy things at my mom and screaming that he wasn't afraid of my dog. We stopped because I wanted to see what his story was and if he needed any help. I was holding Cain's leash tight; but Cain didn't bark, he didn't do anything, even when the guy brought his fist up just shy of Cain's mouth. Cain didn't attack him, it was like he knew the guy was just in trouble and probably needed medication. Paula had been right to insist I get a dog.

My spirits had been bolstered by Cain's arrival in my life, and it was an honor to receive a PRISM Award for my portrayal of Sonny's bipolar condition. The PRISM Awards recognize the accurate depiction of drug, alcohol, and tobacco use and addiction in film, television, interactive, music, DVD, and comic book entertainment. The ceremony was broadcast from the Beverly Hills Hotel on national television and once again I was humbled to accept an award for and grateful to use my art for worthy education about bipolar disease.

But regardless of the positive interlude, if I thought the rough patch had been bad, I had no idea it was going to get much rougher.

One day in the winter I came home to find Paula on the phone, her face drawn, and tears just started pouring out of her. I thought, *She's always the rock, the strong one, it must be bad if she's so upset.*

A friend of Paula's mother's had called to break the sad news to her that Paula's mom had suddenly passed away. We never saw her mother outside of her house and I only went with Paula once a year, if that. But Paula never stopped loving her mother deeply; she still longed for peace to be a part of her mother's life and I know she suffered watching her mom destroy her life with drugs. Paula got to a better place with her mother when the hard drugs faded away, at least enough for Paula to feel like she could be in her mom's life again.

Paula went to her mom's more often after she'd stopped the heavy drugs, to help out with food, cleaning, and picking up the kids to bring them to our house, and later we bought her mom a house in Anza, California, outside Temecula, where she and Paula's adopted sister, Heather, could live. I even ended up getting along with Jean because she had the best sense of humor; she was a really funny person. The tragedy is that even though she tried to turn her life around, she died relatively young—she was only sixty years old. Hard drugs had been her problem when Paula was a kid, but in the end, pills did her in. Paula fought her whole life to have a good, loving relationship with her mother and never really got it; it was always full of pain.

After all that pain and heartache and trying to have a real relationship with her mother, now her mother was gone and had left with no warning. It was so sudden that Paula didn't get to prepare for that loss or say goodbye, and I understood that emptiness and pain. But although Paula was suffering a great deal, her first thought was Heather.

Heather was only fourteen and, like Paula, Heather didn't know her dad and had grown up watching her mother use drugs. To complicate matters, because Paula's mother had adopted Heather from the state, her death meant that Heather immediately became a ward of the state. We would cross that bridge sooner than later, but first Paula had to tell Heather the devastating news. When she met Heather at her school, Paula gently told her that their mom had passed away, and they hugged each other and cried.

I never dreamed we would have another child, but fate had thrown us a twist and we knew we had to adopt Heather. We loved her, and she had nowhere else to go. At the time, Heather was on a treacherous path, and I remember sitting with her one day and sharing some of my own bad choices and telling her she had two choices: the path she was going down, which was bumpy and difficult, and another road, in which she'd have everything she needed.

We knew it was important to let Heather choose, and she decided she wanted us to adopt her. Because Heather was a ward of the state, we had to petition the government, a complicated matter requiring a lawyer to guide the voluminous paperwork through the courts for a year as her case slowly wound its way through the system. But all good things are worth waiting for, and Heather legally became our daughter on April 20, 2009.

One of the most beautiful moments I remember is the day I saw Heather sitting with Paula on the bed, deep in conversation, and I heard Heather ask if it was okay for her to call Paula Mom. One day not long after that she just started calling me Dad, just as naturally as breathing.

While it was a beautiful time, it was also scary when she started hanging out with the wrong people. Heather had seen and gone through a great deal, so, while it took some persuasion, she listened to my urging to begin therapy. I'm so proud that she had the courage to do that, because it allowed her to straighten out her life.

Again, my life on the show mirrored my personal life when in June 2009 Sonny suddenly also had a grown child, but his was one he had never known about. When he left Bensonhurst for Port Charles and a life in the mob, Sonny also left Olivia Falconeri (played by the great and hilarious Lisa LoCicero) behind; he just didn't know that he had also left a child growing in her womb. I think Olivia is probably the one who made the most sense for Sonny to be with—typical Italian mother—but it wouldn't have been as much fun for the audience as the popular Sonny/Carly/ Brenda love triangle.

That's when Dominic Zamprogna came to *General Hospital* to be Sonny's son, Dante, and that entire story line is still one of my favorites. Dominic is a great, solid actor and there were so many layers to that story line. After Dante became Sonny's right-hand guy, Sonny found out he was an undercover police officer there not to become Sonny's successor but to put him in jail for the murder of Claudia Zakara. The fans were thrilled when Sarah Brown returned to play the role of Claudia, and it was so interesting for me to play against her in a completely different role, one that was out to get Sonny. The crowning sequence to the undercover story took place during baby Josslyn Jacks's christening—intercutting back and forth between the church and Sonny and Dante's heated confrontation about Dante's ultimate betrayal of Sonny. As an Italian song played over both a peaceful and violent mash-up of scenes, Sonny shoots Dante point-blank, only to find out when Olivia rushes in that he has just put a bullet in his own son.

Ingo Rademacher plays Jax, who is father to Josslyn, and is also a dynamic part of the other popular Carly/Sonny/Jax love triangle. He is very tall and handsome, with blue eyes and flawless hair—perfect for the role of Jax, the international financier. When Ingo first came on the show, I was very competitive, but he was the perfect nemesis: the bad boy against the prince. Although we're usually mad at each other in scenes, off-camera we joke around a lot.

The one thing Sonny and Jax agree on is protecting and making sure Josslyn, who has lived in Sonny's house, has a good life. Even though he's not her father, Sonny has built a paternal relationship with her. Eden McCoy, who plays Josslyn, is just a pleasure to be around, although her character had already suffered tragic losses at a young age. Those scenes as Sonny guides Josslyn through her grief have been really emotionally charged, and I'm always thinking about my own girls in those moments.

At home, all my kids were in store for another change, and it was life-altering. Paula was very distraught after her mom passed away, and so was her brother, John, who felt terrible guilt that he wasn't there. There was so much left unresolved from their childhoods and I know Paula was struggling with all that, so when she came to me one day and asked if I thought it would be a good idea to move out of Los Angeles, I was all in. We moved to Temecula, a somewhat small town we visited near where her mother had last resided with Heather. Paula found a house high on a hilltop with a beautiful view that seemed to stretch out forever, and I always put my chair out at the edge of the property to meditate surrounded by the gorgeous expanse. The Spanish-style house was built around a huge outside courtyard, and the kids had their own separate wing. There had been no funeral for Paula's mother but when we arrived at the new house, Paula planted lantana flowers—her mother's favorite—in her mom's memory on the hillside, and when they bloomed, Paula took her mother's ashes and spread them among the flowers Jean loved so much.

It was so beautiful and peaceful at our new haven in Temecula that I didn't even mind the commute to Los Angeles. I didn't have a cell phone because I had resisted being tied to one with all my might, but that changed one night when the drive got to me and I actually fell asleep at the wheel. I remember my car hitting something and jolting awake to see that I had run into the side rail. That was another miracle in my life and I thank God my car sustained only minor damage and neither myself nor anyone else was injured. From that day on, Paula made me promise never to drive when I was tired again, even slightly tired. She also went right out and purchased a cell phone for me, so for all my Twitter and Instagram fans, you owe my wife a huge thanks. I probably never would have had my own phone if Paula hadn't insisted.

Paula negotiated a more flexible schedule for me, one where I'd shoot my scenes in three or four days instead of five, so I'd stay in L.A. while shooting them. Tony Geary told me about a friend who was renting a great apartment in L.A., so I checked it out. The place was huge, which was great for Cain and all my brood when the family came to stay in L.A. for events, so I leased the apartment to stay in during the week and I've been commuting this way ever since.

Paula's brother was also still going through a hard time after his mom's death, and Paula wanted him to come to stay with us in Temecula, so John moved there to look after our land and the house. I think Paula will always feel responsible for the tough childhood they had and will always want to protect him.

Although we had moved and started fresh, for all the losses we had endured in such a short time, the worst was yet to come for me. June 18, 2009, I suffered a blow I thought I would never get over, and it's a loss I still feel every single day. One day after buying fresh honey from a guy on the street in Temecula, I walked into the house and when I saw Paula's face I knew something bad had happened.

"Honey, sit down," she said quietly.

"I don't want to sit down, just tell me what's wrong," I said.

"Manny's dead," she gently told me.

I was so angry I couldn't even cry. "What do you mean? How?" I asked.

"He was murdered," Paula said softly, knowing the words were like daggers.

"Fuck!" I yelled.

"He was stabbed eighteen times by a jealous husband," Paula continued slowly.

"I'm gonna kill that motherfucker," I raged. I hadn't talked to Manny for a few weeks because I'd been doing a movie. At the time, he had been in an institution for depression; however, I didn't know that until after he passed, because he didn't want to worry me while I was working—dear, sweet Manny was always concerned about everyone, to the very end.

At Jeff's funeral Manny and I had made a pact.

"When I die, don't have a funeral for me, and I won't come to yours," Manny said.

"I promise," I agreed.

However, Manny's brother, understandably, planned a service, so I talked to his brother and related what Manny had told me after Jeff's funeral, and his brother listened quietly and nodded. He respected our promise to each other and I didn't attend.

Four friends had died pretty much in a row during the past several years and each of them was too young, for each the death was unexpected, and I didn't get to say goodbye to any of them. I started telling people, "Don't get close to me or you'll die." I was aching inside and I threw myself into work, as I always do when I'm depressed. Donna, of course, tried to keep me focused at work, but the weight of all the losses seemed too heavy to handle and I was struggling. To try to get past that seemingly insurmountable roadblock I turned once again to the tool that I had turned to my whole life, and therapy helped me navigate that dark time.

That year, Bridge for a Brighter Tomorrow gave me an award

for raising awareness and fighting the stigma of mental health issues, but I didn't see how tomorrow could be bright, because my guts had been torn out and everything reminded me of the friends I had lost. Although I loved them all, Manny's death hit me the hardest, and after he was gone I picked up the phone ten times a day to call him, then realized he wasn't going to answer. I couldn't accept that he had been taken so violently or that I hadn't been there to protect him like he had always protected me.

Although I didn't cry for anyone at first, the tears eventually come. Out of nowhere, you're hit with a flood of emotions you can't repress, and one day after Manny died, I was running and they hit me like a train coming at full speed, flattening me. I started sobbing and running faster and faster, as if I could outrun the sadness. I of course couldn't, but I ran for several miles until I couldn't run anymore, and even then the tears still flowed. They tell you time heals the sorrow and I prayed for time to pass quickly, but a year went by with every moment as jagged as the one before. Even now, all these years later, it's still a tender wound.

Paula's fortieth birthday also arrived in September after we moved and I knew it was one of those birthdays that hits you more than others, making you think about life, and would take on even more weight now that her mother was no longer around and Paula was still hurting. So I decided it was time for another big surprise. Just as Paula knew I needed animals to help me heal during my grief, I thought it was time to give her a horse that she could get on and ride as fast and as far as she wanted and forget about the world in her happy place.

On Paula's birthday morning, I told her we were going to ride horses. But what I didn't tell her was that I had already bought one for her. It was a beautiful day and as we pulled into a horse ranch in Temecula, she immediately exclaimed how beautiful the paint horse was that was running around the ring. I think the owners were onto the fact that I didn't know anything about horses and had charged me thousands more than the horse was worth, but it was worth it to see her face light up the moment I told her she wasn't just *riding* the paint horse that day, she was the new owner. It was so good to see her smile after all that she had been through.

When she inquired about the horse's name, the ranch owner told us it was Bubba, and Paula and I looked at each other in surprise—our pet name for each other, the one we had inscribed years before on our matching tattoos! If that wasn't enough, when she got up close to Bubba, she saw that he had a tiny heart birthmark and knew why it was meant to be.

Meanwhile, at work, after the culmination of those difficult years losing my friends, Drew Garrett was cast as a new, older Michael to replace Dylan Cash, who had played my TV son since 2002, and I immediately took Drew under my wing. The first scene we did together included six pages of dialogue for him, and I honestly don't know many other actors who could have pulled that off at his age.

"Don't drop the ball, because once it drops, the scene ends," I told him.

I worked with him and he held his own, so one Sunday when Jill called and explained to Paula that they had suddenly replaced him, I was mad. Seeing this kid I had bonded with snatched away without warning was like another loss in the line of losses I had already suffered. I didn't take it well.

The next day I was walking in the hallways at work and when Jill saw me, she could tell I was unhappy.

"What's wrong?" she asked.

"I'm pissed, but hey, it's your show. I just hope this guy's good."

The guy I was referring to is Chad Duell, the brand-new older Michael. I love Chad like a son now, but I was terrible to him for about six months, starting with the first scene we had to do together, which took place in court. Chad's character, Michael, had killed Claudia to protect his mother, and Sonny and Carly had covered up the truth to keep him out of jail. But secrets always come out, and Chad had a long monologue describing how Michael had no choice but to use force to save his mother. He was sweating bullets while I was sitting in the court in front of him just staring a hole through him, and although he did a great job, I didn't talk to him after the scene to tell him that. I was a jerk. Donna was sure to tell me so and helped me come around.

Chad is such a good actor and such a nice guy, I couldn't help but quickly grow to like him and started teasing him like Steve and I tease each other. I began saying before scenes, "Chad, all you have to do is look into my eyes and I'll lead you to the promised land." He even lived at my place in L.A. for three weeks several years ago after a breakup with a girlfriend.

It's not just Chad, however; I'm close to all my TV sons and daughters because they are like family. Watching all these young actors I've mentored go on to achieve so much and garner acknowledgment and awards is satisfying, and when they win an Emmy, I'm so proud it's almost like I'm getting one, too; I feel so invested. Chad has deservedly won Emmys and I can't take any credit for that but I'm still so damn proud of him.

After all the deaths in my personal life, it was finally nice to witness some happiness in life when I watched another friend, Tori Burns, owner of part of the San Francisco Giants' franchise, fall in love and get married. And what a wedding—aside from mine, my favorite of all time, until my own daughters' weddings, of course.

In 2011, Tori married Steve Humphrey, and what made it so cool was where it took place—they exchanged vows at the stadium, right on the field. At the lavish reception under the stadium lights, I sat at a table with Barry Bonds, who played left field for the Giants. At first he was standoffish, but when we started talking, he told me people think he's arrogant but he suffers from anxiety, so when a lot of people are around it kicks in. We connected on that and talked at length and he's a really great guy. Emmitt Smith, running back for the Cowboys, was also seated at our table, and I'll never forget him saying I was more famous than him and everyone at the table arguing about it. He had a point—football players have a helmet on, so it's pretty much a mask hiding their features.

Meanwhile, a high-profile wedding took place in Port Charles as well when Vanessa returned for a while and Sonny and Brenda finally actually tied the knot. It was such a highly anticipated event and fans were so stoked that the wedding was on air for a full week. That same old magic was there, and the ratings were through the roof.

I was also nominated for my sixth Emmy award for my role on *General Hospital*. Sonny's daughter Kristina was beaten up by a boyfriend and landed in the hospital, which led to a very important story line about abuse. As they always do on soap operas, the children grow up far faster than kids do in real life, and two years before, the talented young actor Lexi Ainsworth had been cast as Sonny's now-older daughter. She's another young person who wanted to learn, and so I worked with her as I had the others. She brings a layer of vulnerability to her character that can just break your heart. When I do a scene with her, I'm usually thinking about my own daughters, and it adds that depth to the relationship as well.

As the year came to a close, so did an amazing era—both Jill Farren-Phelps and Bob Guza left the show and in an interesting twist of fate our new executive producer, Frank Valentini, turned out to be the director of an ABC promotional spot I had done as Sonny with Susan Lucci as Erica Kane years before. Although I had not worked with Susan when I was on *All My Children*, in this spot our characters got stuck in an elevator together and it was fun because the whole thing was very tongue-in-cheek. The spot was also highly popular.

When Frank came on board at *General Hospital*, he told me that, of all the people he had to direct for those ads, he was the most scared of me. We had a good laugh about that. By then it was funny to think of people being scared of me—it felt, finally, like that was far from the truth.

CHAPTER THIRTEEN

Celluloid Heroes

People may not realize it, but when Frank took over, we all really thought *General Hospital* was going to be canceled and we would lose our jobs. This was when the O. J. Simpson coverage was at its peak, and when his car chase and subsequent trial took over television, soaps were preempted for weeks and suffered damage from which they've never fully recovered.

The business was also evolving for other reasons. The way everything had always been done, from how we shot to when we shot, all down the line, was revamped to keep up with the new industry dynamics. For the first time I wasn't required to keep such a grueling schedule, and I began to get two weeks off in regular intervals. Now I know why the rest of the world looks forward to summer Fridays!

It turns out Frank was a master at budgeting, and kept the show moving in a cost-efficient manner all while directing some of the episodes. In changing everything he allowed *General Hospital* to stay on the air and everyone to keep working, which in my opinion is a miracle. I love Frank, but I exasperated him sometimes as much as I had his predecessor, Jill, particularly when it came to the character of my on-screen son Morgan.

In 2013, when it was Morgan's turn to rapidly age, one day Morgan was little, and almost the next, he was a teen. I'm the first to admit it now that when I saw Bryan Craig's screen test, I was not impressed. I liked another actor, but the producers wanted to go with Bryan, so Bryan became my new on-set son.

It only took one scene with him to change my mind. It was a party scene and Sonny and Morgan started yelling at each other. As I watched this brand-new kid with his raw emotion and power, I couldn't believe it. He held his own and then some, and I said to myself, *Holy shit, he's the real deal.* One day he asked me if I'd work with him and teach him method acting, and he was like Steve and Vanessa, another diamond, another sponge, taking it all in and making it his incredible own. But even though they had hired Bryan over who I wanted, once he was on the show they didn't support him.

I remember one night in particular when I lost it because I didn't think he was getting the respect he deserved as an actor. It was a dense dialogue scene for him, at least five pages, and all on him because the brilliant Maura West, who plays Ava, didn't have many lines, and I had none. I was in awe of this guy's talent as he blew through that emotional scene, nailing it like a movie star.

But the director just said, "No, do it again."

I loved this director, but I went off. "Why? He was brilliant. None of us could have topped that. I'm not doing it again." But I didn't stop there and I went on, laying into the nonbelievers. "I can't believe how you treat this actor when he's spilling his guts out. I can't wait to leave this place; my contract's up and I'm outta here."

I was so pissed, I stormed off the set.

Now, I had yelled and broken things like a chair before when I was younger and fought harder about every little detail because I thought I was the producer and director back then, but I'd never been as furious as this. As I walked off the stage, our amazing stage manager, Craig McManus, who I love, touched my arm and stopped me.

"You don't want to leave. Your actors are still standing there," he said softly.

He knew me too well, and he was right: I would not desert my actors. I turned around and I went back to the set.

"Maura, Bryan, I'll do the scene again for *you*. But I'm only doing it for you if you want to do it again," I said. We stood there looking at each other for a beat, and in that incredibly tense moment the director had a change of heart and decided against the retake.

The next day I talked to Donna about it, of course. Later, I was in my dressing room with Bryan hanging out between scenes and I told him, "I've always got your back."

When we went upstairs to the set for the next scene, Frank walked in and he was mad. Privately in his office, he laid into me and said it wasn't okay to call them fucking idiots, and that I had to apologize to the crew.

Finally I acquiesced and went back to the set and the amazing crew I absolutely adore because nothing happens without their hard work.

"I'm sorry I blew up last night," I began, but before I could continue, I heard one of their ranks, Jimmy O'Dwyer yell out, "We've got your back, Maurice."

It never happened again and I think things got a little better for Bryan. His character, however, was facing a huge obstacle and Sonny was facing a terrible tragedy. This story line chronicled Morgan's bipolar diagnosis and death, and it's another on my list of best story lines of all time. Watching his character descend into the depths of depression was hard because it hit close to home, but also because I loved this kid and I knew he was going to leave. During the whole arc he asked me endless questions about what it was like to be bipolar. We talked for hours and ran lines and he found so many realistic nuances to incorporate. For one paramount scene, he had a monologue in which he was supposed to spiral out of control.

"You have to talk faster; it's like you're on drugs when you're manic, everything is heightened." I said. "Spit it out like Eminem."

And he did; he sounded like the rapper on steroids and was brilliant to the very last scene, along with Laura, who also did a phenomenal job as a mother losing her son to mental illness and then death. I think the story line was also disturbing for me because at home it was never far from my mind, wondering if one of my kids was going to turn out like me. Thankfully, none of them have exhibited bipolar behavior and I'm grateful, because I wouldn't want them to go through what I've had to experience.

If there's someone in your world whose behavior you may have questions about, a wonderful movie I was involved with that delves into bipolar and its symptoms, among other things, is *OC87: The Obsessive, Compulsive, Major Depression, Bipolar, Asperger's Movie*. The amazing documentary was written and directed by Bud Clayman about his own struggles. Bud's humorous outlook and take on life and all its struggles are inspiring. Bud's a great guy and when he asked me to participate I did, telling my own story in the film and offering insight about bipolar. It premiered at the

San Francisco DocFest and went on to be released in theaters in Los Angeles and New York. After its theatrical release, the International Bipolar Foundation (IBPF) honored me in 2012 with the Imagine Award for empowering others by sharing my story and instilling hope.

Although I was constantly involved with mental health organizations, I still wanted to do more, and in 2013 Paula and I finally decided to make a film about bipolar. We had talked about it for years. We couldn't have done it without Frank scheduling around me so I could have the time off to do it. He didn't really have to agree to because contractually that's at his discretion, but Frank has been great with letting me and the other cast members do work outside the show.

We also couldn't have done it without Steve and Tori Humphrey, because movies cost money, and so does developing them. I will love them forever for believing in us and helping us achieve our goal by investing in our passion project, *The Ghost and the Whale*. Tori recently told me that she was drawn to the project not only because it was inspiring but because she herself has been on medication for severe depression and anxiety for fifteen years, except when she was pregnant and didn't take the medicine. That's why she was so invested not only financially but emotionally.

The film also never would have come to fruition without Paula, because she helped to physically produce it and over three years pushed the never-easy indie boulder up the hill.

First we commissioned a script. Filmmakers Anthony and James Gaudioso are twins I'd worked with on a fantastic film, *Duke*, a few years before, playing a mysterious bad guy named Winky who assaulted a town. Anthony told me a crazy idea about a man who talks to a whale, but he hadn't gotten much further than that. I said, "That's not crazy, that's our movie! I know why he's talking to a whale . . . he's bipolar. That's basically his inner mind, Joseph was in a terrible state of mind." Then Anthony started writing the script about Joseph, a man who is losing his mind because he believes he might have been responsible for his wife's death. His conversations with the whale at the beach about the meaning of life adds a beautiful metaphysical, almost fantastical element to the film. Anthony and James both played leads in the film as well as codirecting it.

We began shooting in February 2013 in Bodega Bay, where the Hitchcock movie *The Birds*, celebrating its fiftieth anniversary at the time, had been filmed, and it was exciting to have Tippi Hedren, the star of that classic, appear as a character in our film. Paula and I had a lot in common with Tippi, because she has dedicated her whole life to the welfare of animals and founded the incredible Shambala Preserve in California, where she rescues lions and other exotic felines from terrible situations. Tori also appeared as a character in the film and it was fun to see Ron Hale and work with him again because it was just like old times.

The first scene took place on the beach in the freezing cold and I thought, *What have I gotten myself into?* As I was standing there in the numbing temperature and wind talking to nothing but the crashing waves, suddenly a seal came out of the ocean and just stared at me, like he knew, like he was worried, and that seemed like a good sign to me.

My favorite scene in the movie was a seven-page monologue in which my character tells the doctor he's invincible while on a manic high. I got more and more jacked up in the scene and after the directors yelled, "Cut!" I heard one of the crew members say, "That was Al Pacino, man!" I could tell, though, by the look on the faces of the two directors they didn't agree.

"Not sure that was enough," one of them said.

I couldn't believe it. I asked Paula what she thought.

She thought they were right. "It wasn't, honey," she echoed.

I resigned myself to the truth and asked the directors, "What do you need?"

They said simply, "Go bigger." But I hesitated, because less always seems like more in a performance, in my book.

"You have to, baby," Paula prodded, but I still wasn't persuaded.

"Baby, listen to me," I said, "I'm already losing my head on this film. How do you know I won't step over a line and never come back?"

She looked at me without any reservations. "Because I believe in you. You can do this."

Seeing her resolve convinced me, so I took another shot at it and this time went even more manic. In every movie there's a moment when you do something and it gets completely quiet and you know you've got the people in your palm, and this was that moment. The entire crew was transfixed and no one moved.

We shot on the remote location for three long weeks. The kids were all there, too, involved. But it was tough, and off-set I was really losing my mind. I yelled at my wife and I yelled at my friend Melissa, who had graciously shown up to help with the production details. I was a time bomb and yet I was on my meds, which made it worse. The last day of filming was also my fiftieth birthday, so when Paula threw a combination birthday/wrap party with music and a big cake I thought it was sweet, but I was so ready to get home I couldn't wait for the party to be over.

What was making me so crazy?

Part of it was the intensity of the role and the dark places I had to go to in order to portray Joseph's decline, but once we were back in Temecula, the dark fog still hadn't lifted. In fact, it had gotten worse. After several weeks, I knew I had to find another therapist. I had been on Dr. Drew Pinsky's HLN show to talk about bipolar disorder in 2011 along with Catherine Zeta-Jones and Patty Duke, so we called him and Dr. Drew found a great person for me to work with.

Just like any other time I'm down, I used acting as a form of therapy and took my depression into work to let it work for me. You can't stop doing what you're doing or you get into a hole, I know because I've been there, and the other alternative—ending it—is not an alternative. You have to keep telling yourself that day by day it will get easier. So I exercised, went to work and therapy, and called Paula at night from my apartment in L.A. because I needed to hear her voice.

In August 2014, Paula incredibly put together a screening of our film followed by a Q and A with the cast and directors at the Writers Guild in Beverly Hills, and I was a wreck. There were five hundred people there, including my *General Hospital* castmates. In my insecure mind, I thought it was too extravagant, which was typical of Paula. But I didn't think it went well. I was certain everyone hated the film and were lying when they came up to say that they liked it.

My problem is I define myself by social media or compliments. This goes back to everything having to be perfect when I was growing up and the bar being set very high. Fortunately or unfortunately, my social media thrives and is positive, but it shouldn't matter either way. I'm working hard on not worrying about what people think, but it's definitely a work in progress. It drives Paula crazy that I'm always posting videos because she would prefer that my face not stay buried in the phone when I'm off work. My daughter Cailey even called me out on it and at first I didn't understand and thought no one was being supportive.

In 2015, an opportunity came up for me to play the character Ridge in the film *Joy* with one of my idols: Robert De Niro. Although I wasn't in a deep funk, there was still a major problem—I hadn't gotten on a plane in ten years. There was no way around it, it was time to confront my panic attacks on a plane, because if I didn't fly to New York I would miss the chance, and I might not get another. It was overwhelming and my anxiety was through the roof. I tried everything but I couldn't get my head in a good place and I couldn't sleep. When I told Paula I couldn't go, she just looked at me. Usually Paula has this sweet, caring voice, but there's this other voice—the firm, "that's it, you're going" voice—and she used it that day.

Cassidy and Joshua accompanied us and when we got to the airport, I boarded the largest plane on the planet, but of course I didn't think it was big enough. It felt like a tiny box to me and I glanced at the exit, but before I could move toward it, Paula touched my arm.

"You're not getting off the plane," she said with finality in that firm voice that I knew I couldn't ignore.

I looked at Joshua and Cassidy, who were already in their seats, and I flashed to the last time I had made my kids get off a plane and miss a trip. I couldn't do that to Joshua or Cassidy again, so I sat down and said a prayer, and although I was anxious, somehow I got through it.

The first day I arrived on the set it was closed to everyone but a few actors and crew. I couldn't tell if one of the guys was the director, David O. Russell, or not, because his face was covered with a surgical mask. It reminded me of Michael Jackson and I thought, *Okay, this guy is weird*, but as it turns out he was sick and didn't want to spread germs to his cast and crew. And then I heard a voice behind me and turned to see Jennifer Lawrence.

"Hi, I'm Jennifer, it's nice to meet you," she said, smiling, and we chatted. She's lovely, and I think she did a phenomenal job as Joy in the film.

The highlight, of course, as well as the terror, was meeting De Niro. In the film there's a world within Joy's world, and the soap opera that her mother follows and Joy's reality bleed into each other, which was really a cool concept. The first scene I had to perform in included Bradley Cooper, Jennifer, and De Niro. I remember watching De Niro watch me, and I was more nervous than I had ever been in any pressure-cooker situation before. He just stared at me the entire scene as I said my lines, but afterward he shook my hand and I felt a huge weight lift off my shoulders, like I had passed on to another sphere at that point. If I did nothing else in my career, I had gotten one perfect day acting in a room with one of my heroes.

Funnily enough, my path crossed Susan Lucci's on the set of *Joy*; on the last day of shooting, I had a scene with her, Donna Mills, and Laura Wright.

"Yell at her! Now tell her you love her!" David Russell interjected different instructions every few seconds. Suddenly the director of photography told him the film had run out, so I thought that was that, but David didn't hesitate. "Put another one in," he directed, and we kept on going.

He said in a TV interview that "soap actors are like professional athletes" and that I "was like the Brando of soap operas" and that means a lot to me, but it's funny, he never got my name right.

"Mike, let's try this," he'd say. I'd follow his instructions, then he'd throw something else at me. "Mitch, do this."

People kept correcting him, but I laughed and told him, "I don't care what you call me."

He smiled and said, "I always forget everyone's name." I get it; I'm pretty bad at names, too. He might've been bad with names, but he sure knew his job—the film was released that December and went on to win a Golden Globe for Best Picture.

After I shot the film, I returned to Port Charles to find that *finally* Sonny was going to save the day. With Frank's approval, the writers wrote an episode where everyone is on *The Haunted Star*, dressed to celebrate, unaware that a bomb has been placed there and is counting down to annihilation. When they detect the device it is too late to disarm it; however, right before the bomb goes off, Sonny grabs it and dives from the boat into the water. For once, Sonny saved lives instead of threatening them, but the haters immediately thought it was overkill and beat us up, complaining that now Sonny had rescued the whole town all at once. Still, I'm glad Frank let Sonny have the moment.

Sonny had a moment with Ava—rather, a grief-driven one-night stand—that resulted in a daughter but didn't erase their seismic hatred for each other. Ava and Sonny's daughter, Avery, are played by twins Ava and Grace Scarola and I have a lot of fun teasing them.

I was finally exploring my own personal layers, and allowing myself to be truly, publicly vulnerable. In February 2016, I was asked to appear on *Dr. Oz*, and this time, with Paula by my side, I allowed myself to be vulnerable and become emotional when talking about bipolar.

At the end of the long, intense interview, they surprised me with a pre-taped video from Bryan, my TV son, which brought tears to my eyes. He said he couldn't have done the bipolar arc without me and my honesty and strength were an inspiration. His sentiments will always mean the world to me.

Finally, finally, I felt like I'd shown the world my true self.

CHAPTER FOURTEEN

God Only Knows

When I was fifty-three, dark days really hit and my personal and professional worlds were rocked to the very core. It started when I was offered a script for an indie film in New York I wanted to do because the concept was really cool: they planned to shoot it in *one* day—*and in a single continuous take.*

I committed to it immediately, but deep down in my gut I also immediately had reservations. It was *General Hospital*'s fiftieth anniversary year and my work schedule was more intense than usual because I had a full five-day week and had dozens of scenes, which made for long work days and dozens of pages to memorize every night. I was giving it my all and then some.

As a soap actor I have to memorize a lot of dialogue and a lot of pages every single night because it's a talking gig, but there's usually less talking in features. This film was different and it was so dialogue-heavy the script was almost one hundred pages of me talking. Even though I'm used to doing one-take scenes on the show, it started to seem overwhelming to do it all without breaking, in one twenty-four-hour period. Four days after I started studying my lines, I began to feel that familiar panic in my bones. It was crippling and I couldn't sleep for days.

But I was about to get a one-two punch.

Paula had not been feeling well and when Vanessa Marcil talked with her awhile at a function, she was convinced something was wrong and Paula needed to have her thyroid checked. Vanessa pushed Paula to go see her doctor, and while Paula usually takes care of everyone else before herself, this time she listened to Vanessa's advice and made an appointment. I'll always be grateful to Vanessa for that.

A few days after the tests, the physician called with bad news. Paula had thyroid cancer, and to make it worse, they were not sure if the cancer had spread. It was like a swift kick in the gut; I couldn't breathe or function.

I couldn't lose Paula. I couldn't picture my life without her.

Knowing that Carol's treatments hadn't stopped the damn cancer from growing or killing her, I was terrified. My head started spinning and the anxiety wouldn't go away, day or night. I visualized Paula in a coffin and kept going down that dark tunnel of hopeless thoughts.

The hospital scheduled surgery to remove Paula's thyroid in mid-June, and until then we would have to wait and hope and pray for the best. There were all the normal pressures—the kids' school and schedules and problems, running the house, caring for sick animals, managing my career—but she wasn't going to let cancer or anything else ruin any of her plans. She amazes me because, no matter what, she just tackles whatever is happening and moves forward.

Meanwhile, I'd also been cast in the indie movie *Hold On*, playing a music executive, and it was too late to back out of it, but

I was still depressed and the darkness that had started after *The Ghost and the Whale* had followed me there. Paula being diagnosed with cancer didn't help, and although the character I played was interesting and I delivered the goods, no one knew I was hanging by a thread, least of all the director, Tarek Tohme.

During all this time, with everything else going on in our lives, Paula had also been embroiled in finishing the final postproduction touches and financing battles for that costly part of filmmaking on *The Ghost and the Whale*. But in true Paula style she completed post on our film while simultaneously beating the pavement to find distribution, and again, against all odds, she did—the film came out on digital and on-demand through MarVista Entertainment in May 2016. We were probably more relieved than anything to finally put our passion project to rest with a distribution deal, and were glad for the distraction during the most terrifying time of our lives.

A month later, the wait for Paula's surgery was over. It took place without any complications and afterward Paula had to stay at the hospital for radiation treatment, but even though she was released three days later, she had to spend a week away from everyone at home because the radiation was dangerous for others. Meanwhile, I was in Los Angeles, coming to the set every day, and it was hard not to be there for her.

Between scenes and at night I was also studying for the indie film and the anxiety was growing because I was distracted and terrified about Paula's illness and what it meant for Paula, for us, and our kids. I could barely stand the pressure crushing me from all sides. I went to work at *General Hospital* the Friday before the film shoot was taking place and began pacing, and then I began weeping. Donna took one look at me and knew the film was doomed.

"You're not getting on that plane," she said.

Once again, we called Dr. Drew and he set me up with a therapist. When I arrived at her office, she explained that she was going to use a nontraditional type of psychotherapy for my stress and anxiety, called EMDR (eye movement desensitization and reprocessing), which is also used with people who experience PTSD. She turned on strobe lights that flickered back and forth and asked me to follow them with my eyes, and while I concentrated on the lights, she asked me to recall a traumatic event, including all the feelings and physical sensations that accompanied it.

A flood of tormenting memories washed over me. I thought about being a little boy, shaking with terror in bed, afraid to be alone in the dark with the demons that lurked in the shadows. I thought about the anxiety waiting for my father to hit me and him standing over me in a rage with the belt and felt its sting against my skin. I thought about being strapped down in the mental institution, unable to move freely, my wrists raw from struggling, sweat covering my body, terrified of the demons I was sure were coming to take my soul.

After a while, she instructed me to switch to a happy memory, still following the flashes of light, and I thought about the first time I saw Paula and how everything inside me pulled me into the store. I thought about her walking toward me at our wedding and my heart being so full it could burst. I thought about her laughing with the kids and how her smile is contagious and felt the smile on my face . . . but then suddenly her face was in a coffin and I instantly was sucked down into the dark again. The flood of memories was interrupted by the fluorescent overhead fixtures as they clicked on and washed the room in bright steady light.

The strobes had stopped and I had been there an hour and a

half, but I didn't feel any different; the knot of anxiety was still sitting in my gut. However, the therapist looked at me and said I was fine and told me to get on the plane. I thought I had heard her wrong, but there was a huge disconnect because she meant it. The moment I left her office I started sobbing, because I knew I still couldn't get on the plane and I also felt like a failure.

Clearly that therapist wasn't the right person for me, and the moral of the story is, follow your instincts. Every therapist isn't meant for you but if you're in trouble, reach out, talk to one. If that person doesn't fit, find another one, and if you can't talk to a therapist, talk to *somebody*, a loved one, a friend.

Don't ignore it.

Don't hold it in.

Don't feel like a failure.

Paula contacted the indie film director and told him I couldn't do the role after all, and I was devastated but knew it was the right call. The director, in one of those rare Hollywood moments that gives you faith in people, was completely cool and understanding. Even though I didn't have the pressure of the film weighing on me anymore, the anxiety still wouldn't dissipate and was loading me down like a ton of bricks. Two more weeks passed and I still wasn't sleeping, because I was terrified to close my eyes—when I did, I kept seeing Paula's face in that coffin.

This anxiety was a new and more menacing beast, because in the past anxiety would usually leave after minutes or an hour, but not this, and not now.

To distract me, Paula decided we would drive to Vegas with the kids. We had gone numerous times over the years for concerts and boxing matches and I had even met Sugar Ray Leonard in a casino once and welterweight Keith Thurman, too. Vegas was always a fun destination and an easy last-minute road trip for us, but this time I couldn't shake the anxiety, and while everyone hung out in the casino I was in bad shape.

I don't know why, but the anxiety won't go away sometimes, and when it gets that bad, I just have to ride it out, so when we got back to Temecula I stayed in my room for days. I tried to sleep, but the scary uncomfortable feeling always started creeping in to choke me and I would bolt back up, sweating. Now I just try not to fight it, but that's easier said than done, and during that episode the doctor had to prescribe Xanax to knock me out just so I could get some rest.

One night I finally went out, and while I was in a drugstore a woman started talking to me.

"You saved my life. I saw you on *Dr. Oz*," she told me.

I was honest and told her I was suffering right then but that I had to just keep on keeping on. I told her things would get better and I desperately wanted to believe that, but I couldn't see a light at the end of the tunnel because I knew I had to go back to L.A. to work on Monday and I was scared I couldn't do it. I was reading meditation books but that didn't help, and on Sunday night before I had to drive to Los Angeles I was huddled in a corner crying.

When Paula saw me, she took on that firm tone. "Honey, enough. You can do it. You've got to go to work tomorrow."

But I didn't get much sleep and early in the morning I watched church services on television to comfort me. The first thing the preacher said was, "Today we're going to talk about anxiety." I listened and I prayed, but I still didn't want to go back to L.A., so Paula said she would go with me. I felt ashamed that I needed her to be with me and said I could do it myself, but when the time came to get in the car to drive, I couldn't move my muscles to start the ignition. I just sat there for a moment or two with Paula patiently waiting, and then she gently opened the door and helped me out, steering me to the passenger seat.

During the drive I couldn't calm down and when we arrived at my apartment in Los Angeles, once again I couldn't move my limbs to get out of the car. After Paula talked to me awhile, I got out of the car; we walked through the hallways to the door of my apartment, and it was crazy but I couldn't even make myself put the key in the lock. It was surreal, like I was trying to swim in quicksand. Once again, Paula soothed my fears and assured me everything was okay. I didn't want to go inside my apartment, either, and Paula was, as always, ever so patient and talked to me until she convinced me it would be fine to enter. Opening the door, she helped me inside, promising she wouldn't leave me alone that night. It was terrible and it terrified me that the anxiety had gotten such a tight grip on me that I physically couldn't move.

Paula contacted Dr. Friedemann Schaub, a therapist in his forties based in Paris I had found online, and whom I absolutely love. He gave me this beautiful scenario that I use often when he said, "Pretend that your son Joshua is on the bed and he's scared and you come to him and you say, 'I'm here, I'm your dad, I'm going to protect you,' and Joshua gets in your arms and feels safe. Well, imagine that little boy is really you." That has helped me so many times when my anxiety has gotten bad.

This time, over Skype, he taught me a breathing exercise. I take a step, I take a deep breath, and say, "I am confident." He told me to start at the top of the stairs. Breathe, walk another step. Breathe. Go down another stair. Breathe, take another step, another stair.

I am confident.

I am confident.

I am confident.

Breathe.

With this new tool, I was able to make myself go back to work. I practiced the breathing exercise constantly in between scenes and in my dressing room. I had a big story line and there were so many monologues, I wasn't sure if I could get through them. I remember being full of despair and thinking, *They don't know what I'm going through.*

Then I had to go in front of the camera and finish the scenes.

Dominic knew and listened to me while I cried with him, and I also talked with Laura about it and told Frank. It took a while to get through that anxiety period, but, little by little, things do get better, whether you can see the light at the end of the tunnel or not. You just have to keep doing what you usually do, going through the motions. I couldn't stop, even though there were times I wanted to. Even if I didn't do anything else, I still had to take Cain out for exercise two times a day, and some days that alone felt like climbing the tallest mountain in the world, but I did it.

A longtime viewer who suffers from depression once told me that it helps her when she turns on the TV and I'm there, because she knows I have bipolar and struggle like she does and that if I can go to work, she can go to work. I try to remember that and keep on showing up, but during times like this one it's difficult.

During all this time, Paula was sick and still doing what she always does, taking care of me and everyone else. It was months and months, a blur of doctor appointments and medicine and tests and waiting. Always waiting for word that she would be okay. When she started losing her hair and gaining weight from the medication, she stressed about that and threw herself even more into keeping busy with work and everything else.

I couldn't make her understand that no matter what, she still took my breath away, in every sense of the word. She always will.

More than ever, I really appreciated my friends during that time—particularly Donna, who had consistently made herself available as my emotional support. She talked me down many days, when my mind started going to the dark place, imagining life without Paula. Donna made me feel like things would be okay, and I think all my work on my mental health over the years helped me guide the kids through the cancer scare. We all view Paula as being indestructible, and I'm proud of the kids because they handled it so well. They didn't even entertain the possibility of her not getting better.

Me, well, my thoughts went to the worst-case scenario.

It helped to have another friend join the show.

Stephen A. Smith, who is a commentator on ESPN's *First Take*, was back in a new recurring role as Sonny's security expert, Brick Smith. I first met Stephen when he tweeted that he had loved *General Hospital* since watching it as a kid with his grandmother. His cohosts, Max Kellerman and Molly Qerim, surprised him one day by bringing me on the show. But that wasn't the only surprise—I came armed with a scene from *General Hospital* and challenged him to read it with me. He was so good the producers asked him to come on *General Hospital* in a guest role. Talk about charisma, that guy's got it, and then some. Each time he's on the show, they give him more and more to do.

By the fall of 2016, I had been offered the role of a cop, Detective Alvarez, in the Lifetime thriller *A Lover Betrayed*, which shot on election eve in Los Angeles. I liked playing the good guy for a change. Everyone was glued to the election results between scenes to see who would be the new President, assuming it would be the first female President in history, and we were all stunned that it went the other way.

I was also part of the inaugural Deconstructing Stigma: A Change in Thought Can Change a Life campaign, which is an ambitious project featuring a 235-foot gallery in Boston's Logan International Airport between Terminals B and C with wall-sized photographs of people and their own words about their mental health journey to educate the public and change hearts and minds about those who have been diagnosed with bipolar and other mental health disorders. McLean Hospital, the largest psychiatric affiliate of Harvard Medical School, collaborated with Logan International Airport as well as the American Foundation for Suicide Prevention, the International OCD Foundation, the Massachusetts Association for Mental Health, the National Alliance of Mental Illness, and Project 375 to develop the first Deconstructing Stigma campaign, which also included the deconstructingstigma.org website and a coffee table book, which reached millions of people in 2017, and plans are under way to install similar exhibits at other airports. When you actually walk through the airport and see the faces of everyday people next to famous faces, all sharing the same stories in the hopes of destigmatizing mental illness, it's more powerful than you can imagine.

Not long after, I got a call one day from Ryûhei Kitamura, a notable Japanese director, for a role in a feature film called *Nightmare Cinema* that was shooting in February 2017. Now, I'm not big on horror movies and I hadn't been interested in doing one, but this was an interesting concept because it was several small movies within one larger movie. But the real catch was that Mickey Rourke, who was an idol of mine ever since I'd seen him in *Diner*, was playing a role that spanned all of them.

Each segment also had different cool directors, including Alejandro Brugués, Joe Dante, Mick Garris, David Slade, and Ryûhei, who was helming the segment entitled *Mashit*, which centers around a priest, Father Benedict. Steve Bauer was originally cast in the role, but his mom had just passed away and he understandably had to pull out of the film. The director wanted to meet, so we set up a time and we hit it off immediately, and the next day they offered me the role of Father Benedict. I relished playing something completely different from all the roles I'd done so far, and my own journey with God and the devil made it even more fascinating, but I always get the sense that I'm the soap guy coming in and they think I'm less than or not good. That first day I know I have to prove their misconception is wrong and I do, I show them I can do it in one take.

I went to rehearse the first scene dressed as the monsignor, and believe me, when you put on that priest outfit you really do feel differently and it impacts how you move. I also flashed to that iconic movie that had scared me so much as a child, and it was hard to believe I was playing a priest doing an exorcism in a movie after *The Exorcist* had terrified me so much. When Mickey didn't show up, Ryûhei explained Mickey's a method actor and there would be no rehearsal and since I'm a method actor, too, I was good with that.

Eventually Mickey came on set wearing a long leather coat with no shirt, and let me tell you, that guy is buff.

"What scene is this?" he asked, then he looked at me. "Is this the kid I'm working with?"

"No, he's the priest," the director responded.

I have to admit I was a little nervous working with someone I respected so much, so I focused on the scene, which put my character in harm's way . . . to put it mildly. Mickey's character is vicious and evil and Mickey was equally intent; he never breaks character for a beat. We did a second take, then a third, and Mickey grabbed my face and hit me really hard, but when Ryûhei yelled, "Cut!" instantly Mickey transformed into a concerned, caring guy.

"You all right, man?" he asked. "Was that too hard?" I shook my head no, and he extended his hand. "Hi, I'm Mickey Rourke," he said with a smile. Although he just couldn't talk to or deal with me as his character, he ended up being so nice to me.

After I shot the film, I took part in the seventy-fifth anniversary celebration of Didi Hirsch Mental Services at the Erasing the Stigma Awards, presenting the Leadership Award to writer/director Paul Dalio, whose film *Touched with Fire* was inspired by his own experience. It explores the relationship between mental illness and creativity via two young characters with bipolar who fall in love after they are hospitalized. Judy Collins, who lost her son to suicide, and Anna Akana were also honored that day.

Although I'm always there to support Didi Hirsch Services, my wish and hope is that one day there will be no need for the Erasing the Stigma Awards. I pray for the day that I won't get a call to be a presenter or receive another trophy for educating people about what it's like to live with bipolar, because one day I hope we completely eradicate the stigma that torments people with mental illness.

Another wish—and one that came true—was that the doctors declared Paula cancer-free. The long, long period of waiting through almost two years of appointments and tests and more tests finally came to an end. I'll never forget that day as long as I live. It's like the darkest cloud that I could ever imagine had lifted. I've never been so happy, so relieved, so thankful.

Having to take thyroid medicine for the rest of her life is a hefty price to pay, and Paula sometimes experiences discomfort, but you'd never know it—she is unstoppable and plows right on through life without missing a beat. She really is incredible.

God only knows what I'd be without her.

CHAPTER FIFTEEN

The Godfather Waltz

There was more to celebrate. The year 2018 marked my twenty-fifth anniversary on *General Hospital*, and what felt like a lifetime since I had stood on the set at the beginning, hearing voices. It had been decades since I, without medication, had had a full-blown mental breakdown.

So much had changed in my head and heart and life.

I had evolved from the macho guy who made bad choices. I had married my soul mate. I had repaired the damaged relationship with my father and become a father myself. I had learned to accept my disease and manage it with meds so I wouldn't have breakdowns. I had faced my demons and learned a lot about myself in therapy. I had found my voice.

I had also learned that what you want and what you need are different. I had started out obsessed with becoming Al Pacino, being a movie star, finding fame, fortune. Career success and awards aside, I had found that the real purpose for me on earth is teaching young actors and sharing my story about mental health with others—and using the voice I'd discovered to erase the stigma. It gives me a deep sense of satisfaction, more than any role I've ever gotten, more than any award bestowed.

I wasn't the only one who had changed over the years. Sonny had changed a lot, too.

One day Frank said to me, "You're gonna sing."

I laughed. "Sonny don't sing," I said emphatically.

But Frank continued, "It's for Mike. He won't be able to remember the words and you're going to finish the song."

Sonny's father, Mike, had returned to town and sadly started showing signs of Alzheimer's. Max Gail took over the role the amazing Ron Hale had played for sixteen years before leaving the show.

How could I say no to Frank's request? Sonny wouldn't.

It turned out Sonny wasn't singing at the famed Nurses' Ball fans look forward to every year, where the cast members showcase their singing and dancing skills and AIDS awareness also takes the stage. He was re-creating a memory for his father in a club where Mike used to sing, to help him hang on to his memories. You can always convince me to do it if it's a good story—and this one was a *really* good story.

Working with Max stirred up a lot emotionally for me from the moment he auditioned. He showed up with long hair and a beard, but from the minute we started reading the scene I felt a deep bond and I knew. At the end he kissed me on the forehead and I cried.

After he left, Frank said, "He's Mike."

I said to Frank, "I can't do this."

Frank looked at me and said gently, "You have to." He knew why it was emotional for me. Aside from the devastating Alzheimer's story line that would wrench us all for the next year, once the long hair and beard were gone, everything about Max was my dad—they could have gotten the hat, the trousers, the jacket, all of it out of my dad's closet.

Right then, things were tough with my own father. H.J. called to report that Dad had been falling; he thought the house we had grown up in was just too much for my parents, too many steps and too much space for them to handle alone. So we started talking to them about selling the house and moving. At first my father didn't want to. Giving up everything you know and all that independence is hard. I understood his resistance.

While we were having these discussions, I was reliving some of those same themes in scenes at work about aging and losing independence and healing old wounds between father and son when Mike moved in with Sonny and Carly. One particular scene almost broke me. When Mike has to tell Sonny he's ready to go live in the memory facility, I started crying—it was that ugly crying, and I just couldn't control myself, so we had to stop the scene and shoot it later.

Max brought so many layers to Mike and such humanity and dignity to Mike's struggle with Alzheimer's. Since Sonny and Mike had always had a contrary relationship, Carly was the bridge between them in that story line and Laura did an amazing job threading that needle. It was hard to get through a lot of scenes; it hit close to home because I was watching my father, both my parents, age, and that gives you a totally different perspective on life.

The story line was brilliantly written to showcase the complicated layers of the issue for the person afflicted and everyone who cares about them. As memory starts to fade, it's terrifying for everyone—there's anger, denial, and painful but necessary decisions to make. Eventually the terrible day comes when the person who is ill looks at relatives and doesn't recognize them. The work really educated me, and we got so much love from fans for the story line. So many people told me their stories about watching their loved one slip away, saying the show helped them feel less alone dealing with it. I'm honored that my twenty-fifth year on the show took on an issue that touched so many people. That makes my list of top favorites.

While I was embroiled in facing the reality of those you love aging on and off the show, I was also watching my constant pal Cain turn into an old man. Once my amazing dog turned ten, he started moving slower and showing signs that he didn't feel well. We took him to the vet and found out he had a heart problem— fluid kept building up around it. We put him on meds but I couldn't take him back to Los Angeles with me anymore because the car ride was too long and hard on him. Those rides became so lonely without my buddy riding shotgun.

Every morning at home in Temecula, I'd sit in my chair and have coffee and Cain would sit with me. One weekday while I was in Los Angeles working, Cain slowly made his way to my chair. Even though he was really sick and it was hard for him to walk far, he labored all the way from the back of the house and lay down by my chair like he was waiting for me.

And then he was gone.

When Paula called me to tell me, it hit me harder than any animal I've ever lost. I couldn't bear to run where we used to take our walks or not see Cain waiting at the door with that look on his face when I opened it. Like always, I distracted myself from the pain with work, and as always, Donna was there to talk to and help me gain perspective. She knew how I related to Cain more than I did with most humans, because she was the same way. She knew how hard it was for me to let go.

Landing my next film not long after was bittersweet, because I got the opportunity through a woman I met by sheer coincidence *because* of Cain.

One day years earlier, I was walking Cain and a stranger was so taken with him that she had to stop and flag me down. We started talking, and as it turned out, J.R. Stewart was also a producer. We became friends and she sent me many scripts over the years, the most recent for the movie *Equal Standard*, starring Ice-T.

Even though I had major anxiety the night before, I got on the plane to New York in June 2018 for the shoot in Queens. I loved the director and it was a nice role, but I remember it was so hot on the jail set I thought I was going to have heatstroke.

As the months went by, I still missed Cain every day, so I was relieved to get another great role outside of *General Hospital* to keep my mind busy. My agent called and said Lifetime wanted me to audition for the role of John Gotti in *Victoria Gotti: My Father's Daughter*, based on Victoria's best-selling memoir. Victoria wrote the script and was also the executive producer, so living up to her father's image would be an interesting challenge, I thought. Who wouldn't want a chance at that role?

To audition, since I was in Los Angeles at the apartment alone, I had to hold the camera to tape myself saying the lines, which is always tricky, but I felt good about the result and sent it to Paula. After she watched it, she called me.

"Honey, you need the accent," she advised.

"I ain't doing more accent." After we argued about that for some time, I finally did a reading making the accent strong, and Paula sent the audition tape in to New York. The next day they hired me. I heard later, however, that it was actually Victoria's mother who pushed to cast me.

As the story goes, Victoria asked her mother, who she's named after, "Who can play my father?"

Her mother said, "Only one person can do that. It's the guy who plays Sonny on *General Hospital*."

As it turns out, not only was Victoria's mother a fan of the show, but she had sent me a letter years ago, talking about her son being bipolar and all the struggles they'd had, and I had written her back to encourage her. She still has that letter, which means a lot to me.

After they called to tell me I was going to play the role of Gotti, I only had forty-eight hours to age ten years, gain weight, and get a Bronx accent, so you can guess what I did—I ate as much as I could and started worrying about the accent. There isn't a lot of film out there with John Gotti speaking, but I did find a clip of his voice on YouTube, which I listened to over and over.

We flew from beautiful eighty degrees August weather in Los Angeles to Canada, and when we landed it was freezing outside. I immediately met with the costume designer to get Gotti's wardrobe down, and the minute I started trying on all these great clothes and wearing them I couldn't help but carry myself differently. Like a mobster. Like Gotti.

As I was walking to the bathroom, a small woman with a huge smile greeted me. "Hi, what's your name?"

I introduced myself. "Hi, I'm Maurice."

"I'm Catherine Cyran, I'm your director." She smiled again.

Catherine is dynamite in a tiny package and we clicked from the get-go. It was the same with Chelsea Frei, who played Victoria, and Gotti's kids—Zoey Siewert, who was young Victoria; Micaela

Nyland as young Angel; and Andre Anthony as John Gotti, Jr. We all bonded and they did a fabulous job. The first thing Chelsea told me was that she watches *General Hospital* and so does her mom, and the kids echoed that same sentiment.

I spent a lot of time in Victoria's trailer gathering as much first-hand information about her family as I could. Her husband was bipolar and we talked about that, and I also gleaned so many details about her father. The first thing she said to me, emphatically, was, "Don't play my dad like Tony Soprano but like Michael Corleone."

The table reading with the cast, Victoria and the other producers, and Catherine was nerve-racking because I was wondering how much accent I should use, and on top of that one producer was very cold to me. It didn't help that the first day of shooting I couldn't get the accent right, but thank God they weren't covering me and the camera was on Chelsea. I could feel the mood in the room and the producer wasn't happy, so I was petrified because my close-up was next. Mercifully, we broke for lunch and I sat in the car with Paula, quiet for a few minutes, until finally I said, "I don't know, baby, I can't get it."

But Paula knew I could and took me to the trailer, running lines over and over and over until finally something clicked, and when we returned to the set after lunch break to shoot my close-up the accent was there. Catherine gave me a thumbs-up and we continued to the next scene, where Gotti and his wife are fighting in front of the kids and she comes at him with a knife. I remember when I first yelled at her everyone jumped and it got quiet, and I knew in that moment I had it.

The following day we shot the last scene of the film, a terribly touching and sad scene between Gotti and his daughter. In it,

Victoria visits Gotti in prison to find he is dying of cancer, and all the things they've never said to each other sit between them like a huge wall. It was draining emotionally because I was thinking of my own daughter Cailey and wishing I could have told her more that I was proud of her for going to college.

The same producer always talking to Paula or the director to complain, however, was upset that I wasn't playing Gotti like Tony Soprano. It was exhausting and confusing because there were two different mindsets about this character, but Victoria seemed like the honest authority on the subject to me, so I followed her lead. She told me countless stories about her dad, and seeing him through her eyes informed my performance.

In the first couple of scenes I had ignored the dialect coach and the accent was okay, but after five days off I called the dialect coach. "Help!" I pleaded, and the coach did; after that, the accent got better.

But the real problem was the producer who clearly didn't want me in the role and made it miserable for me. Thank God for Victoria, and my brilliant director, Catherine, who communicated with me, believed in me, and balanced it out. At least three times I told Paula, "Put me on a plane; I'm outta here," but Paula always talked me down and I got through it, although it was unpleasant. In a way, I believe all that negativity from the producer ignited me to perform better. In every scene there was so much angst inside me I channeled Gotti's rage more because of how I was feeling.

Gotti was the hardest thing I had to do in my career, because I have never wanted to quit a film and I wanted to quit that one. But I didn't. I worked my ass off, listening to "Gives You Hell" by the All-American Rejects every day, and pushing through.

My psychiatrist, Dr. Schaub, took one look at me over Skype and said, "You're calm, you're level, and I think this experience has changed you."

I think he was right. I think after everything that had happened the past several years, Gotti should have been the breaking point, but it wasn't, because each tragedy had changed me, little by little. I had learned, really learned, to use all the tools I had been gathering all these years. Paula always told me I could overcome anything, and for the first time I thought she was right.

But it took a lot out of me. When we finished shooting, I was spent. Sonny is like being in first gear and Gotti was like being in third gear and I couldn't wait to get back and see everyone at *General Hospital*. We left at one o'clock in the morning and flew to Los Angeles, and when we landed I drove straight from LAX to the set to do a scene with Steve.

"Take that John Gotti out of here," he said in the middle of the scene, because I was still doing the damn accent.

It was also good to be back because Frank had planned a twenty-fifth anniversary tribute show for Sonny and me. The episode was really something special, entitled "What If?"—what would have happened if Sonny had never killed anyone as a young boy and gotten trapped in the mob? It felt like a huge movie set with all the extra bells and whistles they brought in for the shoot that examines Sonny's life choices. Dominic had been off the show a little while but came back for that episode, and that meant a lot to me. I also knew the brilliant director Phideaux Xavier would make it special.

This tribute show was extra-special because it was also a family affair. What better child to capture the inner turmoil of Sonny (and me) than my own incredibly talented son? Although he had been in our film *The Ghost and the Whale* in flashbacks, he'd had no lines or scenes interacting with other actors. I knew he thought it was fun, but I had no idea he wanted to act until one day when I was working at the house with Franky Cammarata, the brother of Cassidy's boyfriend, an actor who at the time was a model just starting out. He wanted help for an audition, and Joshua, thirteen, was watching. Franky tried but just couldn't get it.

"Hey, Dad, let me try it," Joshua said.

"Okay, go for it."

I really had no expectations, but I was stunned at how good he was. He came at the scene from a totally different direction, without any coaching, and it was raw and instinctual. He also really got into it and I could see him light up. That look was familiar. It reminded me of how I felt when I discovered what I wanted to be in life.

"I want to act, Dad," he announced on the spot.

Of course I felt a burst of pride that my boy wanted to follow in my footsteps. "Okay," I said. "But you have to be grateful, buddy. God gave you a talent for so many things—acting, piano, boxing—but if you don't have the drive to back it up, it won't matter. Determination outweighs talent. So thank God every day for yours and don't waste it."

He's got more talent than me; thank God I have the drive and will to make it happen.

Talk about being proud when Frank hired him. That was a special moment and it was pretty cool to perform with Joshua, particularly watching him as a younger version of my character. Max Gail was also in the scenes, and he and Joshua and I were all soaking wet from a rain machine making the soundstage feel very much like a cold, dreary day in upper New York. Joshua held his own and was amazed that he got to shoot a prop gun in the scene. Ironically, he also had to be soaking wet most of the day, just as in his last acting job on our film *The Ghost and the Whale*, because in the episode Sonny sees his younger self standing outside his window in a rainstorm. But again, Joshua didn't complain about being cold even though he walked around wrapped in a blanket between scenes.

My daughter Heather was sitting on a barstool in one scene and Cailey and Cassidy's pictures were framed on Sonny's mantel as his children in his alternate life. Paula, Cassidy, and my parents were all watching from behind the camera and I felt so blessed. It was one of those magic days.

Meanwhile, I continued to talk to my own father about selling their house in Martinez and suggested they come live with us. Simultaneously, Paula also started looking for another house for us that would accommodate my parents as well.

We searched for months and we finally found a beautiful house outside Temecula. The first thing I saw was a large pond against a backdrop of huge boulders with a perfect view of serene trees and hills stretching for miles, with plenty of land for our horses. The massive stone fireplace, high ceilings, and natural light flooding the interior of the house also won me over.

We purchased the house and finally convinced my parents to sell theirs. We built a separate wing for my parents and they made that their own home. Just as when I was little, everything is beautiful and always perfectly in its place. My mother keeps every piece of memorabilia from our lives and has bookcases of scrapbooks to prove it, and the guest room in their wing has framed photographs of me and my brother from floor to ceiling. It's a constant reminder to me how much she loves me and my brother and how

Maurice Benard

much she supported me every step of the way on the path toward achieving my dream of acting.

It's like everything has come full circle. Dad and I sit on the couch and watch the 49ers and boxing like we did when I was growing up, but of course things are different now; all of my anger at him has faded away. Even in his eighties, he goes to my appearances at clubs and gets up onstage with me to sing to the crowd, like I used to sing to his guests at parties. My fans love that as much in real life as they do on my Instagram.

The older I get, the more perspective I have, and now I'm grateful for every day I have with my parents and for every day they are healthy. My mother and father helped me when I was at my lowest, my darkest, my worst, and didn't stop loving me. They did the hardest thing a parent can do and committed me to an institution to get help. They found Dr. Noonan for me, and the lithium that saved me.

Because of their belief in me and their help, I was now equipped to help my mother when she decided to confront her own anxiety and depression.

We had never discussed it all these years I had been dealing with my own. I had never thought about it when I was younger, but as I got older and went through therapy, I thought back over the years to how anxious she was when I went to school the first time, and how anxious she was when I was involved in sports matches, and so many other situations. I just hadn't put two and two together until we were living in the same house again and I saw her every day.

I started noticing that anxious, dark energy more and more, so I went to my dad and told him I thought she was going through something and we had to help her. He agreed, and one day we all sat down together.

"Mom, it seems like there's something inside you that's dark and ugly, I think you're depressed and suffer from anxiety. I'm telling you this because I love you and want to help you," I said gently but firmly.

I was surprised when my mother suddenly opened up.

"Hijo, I'm tired of living like this, I'm tired of living with nerves all the time. I hate the way I feel inside," she blurted out bluntly.

My mother is smart and intuitive and I think all these years she knew she was dealing with depression and anxiety but she didn't feel like she could say anything. That's generational and cultural, just like her response to my dad's affairs, which luckily they worked through.

I took her hand and led her outside and we sat meditating and breathing in the peaceful surroundings.

As I talked about the importance of therapy and how much it would help, she listened and the tears started forming. "I want to feel better, hijo," she finally said with conviction.

I'm so proud of her. It's a beautiful thing to be able to better yourself and change, and when you're in your eighties, it's downright amazing. She's starting her own journey to her own self-discoveries and I'm right there for her, just like she was there for me as I went on my long dark journey.

There was much to be thankful for. As the fall arrived, we planned a huge Thanksgiving feast at the new house and invited friends and family.

If family is God's best gift, true friends are a close second. Even though the house was still under construction—the kitchen floor hadn't even been finished—no one cared. Friend after friend only seemed to see the food and wine and enjoy laughing and catching up. They were also thrilled to meet my new animals. Since I still missed Cain so much, as always Paula knew an animal would help heal me. That's how Buddy the Goat, another Instagram star, came to live with us, along with three alpacas, two more horses, and two maremmas. I spend my mornings with my coffee outside with them.

Paula and my dad and Cassidy cooked all day and my father was the bartender as people began arriving. After it got dark, the guests sat at long tables hugging the walls of the circular turretesque room in the center of the house under its vaulted ceiling, with dish after dish of delicious food Paula had prepared on a table in the center of the room. While everyone piled food on their plates and laughed, I looked at all the people who were in my life, gathered to celebrate the amazing gift of friendship. I was moved and grateful, and I stood on my chair to tell everyone there how much they meant to me and my family.

I also thought about all the people who weren't there, but one person in particular was on my mind. Donna had been sick and hadn't been at work for weeks. I didn't realize how long she'd been sick. Looking back, it's clear she had known when I talked to her on my cell phone at the airport waiting to board my flight to Canada for the Gotti film.

"How are you feeling, Donna?" I asked.

"Oh, my stomach's bothering me, so the doctor's doing some tests. But it's nothing. Now, don't you be nervous, you are going to kill this role," she said.

Some friends stayed overnight and helped me feed Buddy the Goat in the morning. As we hung out in the kitchen drinking coffee and swapping stories, I got a text that Donna, my dear friend, was not doing well. It turned out that when we last talked, she was aware she had bile duct cancer but didn't want to worry me because she knew I was nervous. That was typical Donna.

She hung on for another week, and on December 6 we got a call that Donna was gone. Donna and I were as close as could be, and receiving that call was like a family member had been taken. As with all my other friends I'd lost before her, I didn't get to say goodbye to Donna. She didn't want me to see her that way; she was protecting everyone to the very end.

It was strange to think Donna wasn't at home or coming back someday for just one more irritating hug. But this time when tragedy struck, the darkness didn't come for me and I didn't go into a spin. It was almost as if Donna were out there, like an angel, wrapping me in that calm. Paula and I attended a memorial for Donna at her church in Los Angeles and everyone from *General Hospital* showed up, and it was clear by the packed church that she was loved by so many people. Her send-off was touching, peaceful, and beautiful, and I could feel her spirit present all around us.

At the studio, Frank unveiled a bench with a plaque lovingly dedicated to Donna in her memory. It sits just outside the set where she always took her breaks to soak up some sun, and her husband Nick and I were the first to sit there that day. Nancy Lee Grahn and the wonderful Jane Elliot, who has played Tracy Quartermaine for decades, joined others in creating a GoFundMe page for Donna's sons Nick, Jr., Vito, and Antonio in honor of our beloved Donna. The new story line after she passed also honored her: Sonny and Carly's new baby is named Donna Courtney Corinthos (Courtney after Sonny's deceased sister). I had to give a long speech about the "girl from the neighborhood" who inspired the name, and it was one of the hardest monologues I've ever had to do. As I described

Donna to a T it was emotional for everyone in the scene and on set. I know that Donna is smiling at that namesake.

A week after Donna died, her son Nick, Jr., came to the studio to see me. He had always suffered from anxiety and Donna discussed that many times with me, and whenever she asked me to reach out and talk to him, I did. She was always so strong for everyone.

When he walked in, I asked him how he was and he said he felt a peace, and I told him I felt it, too, for the first time in my life.

"I think it's your mom giving us this gift," I said.

He nodded in agreement. "I think so, too."

Not long after, Donna's husband, Nick, Sr., came out to the house and hung out with the goats and we talked about Donna for hours. The thing that sticks with me most is that Nick kept saying he didn't know how he was going to live without her. He knew he had to be there for his three boys or Donna would "kick my butt from heaven," but he was having a hard time with it, and just six months later he passed away. I hope Donna's not too mad at Nick because he couldn't be there for the boys. I think he needed her more and I understand how he felt. I also know Donna made sure she gave her boys the strength they needed to handle this; I think that's a fact.

The last time Nick, Sr., and Donna had been at our new house together was right before Donna got sick. He loved the pond and kept teasing that he was going to fill it with fish. It was a beautiful day and after we hung out awhile we went out to dinner. We laughed and had a great time. I had no idea that was the last time I'd be together with them, or the last happy memory I'd create with them. I will always treasure it.

CHAPTER SIXTEEN

The Future's So Bright, I Gotta Wear Shades

I haven't cried yet for Donna, but I still feel her around. She radiated a sense of peace and calm, and dealing with the grief of losing her in a healthy way is proof of the gift she gave me. That peace I felt after the funeral followed me into the new year, and all the demands of my schedule didn't affect it.

In January I had a big personal appearance facing me and had to get on a plane to Memphis. In the winter. Usually that could have been a big problem for me and caused a lot of stress and anxiety, but although the weather was bad and caused terrible turbulence during the flight, somehow I wasn't terrified like many of the other passengers.

The *General Hospital* fan event at Graceland was probably the biggest event we'd ever had and was also the first time the cast had stayed at the same hotel with all the fans. The new hotel Priscilla Presley meticulously designed and decorated was really stunning. Paula is a huge Elvis fan, so she was thrilled to go, and Cassidy was with us, as well as a few friends who ended up helping me sneak to the restaurant or the gym or to get in and out of the hotel without getting mobbed by the fans.

It always amazes me that fans are willing to travel some distance to attend such events—sometimes, for the international travelers, thousands of miles. I talked to people who were there because the trip was an anniversary gift, or it was a birthday wish, or groups of girlfriends had planned it as their ultimate girls' weekend out. No matter who I talked to, there were interesting stories from all over the country, and even a few international travelers.

I think the craziest moment during that event (outside of seeing Paula at the Elvis museum!) was putting on a hoodie and sneaking down to the ballroom late one night where the fans were gathered to watch favorite episodes of *General Hospital* on a big screen. The idea was to come in the back and just sit in the audience until someone noticed I was there and give them an unscheduled surprise appearance and selfies with me. We snuck through the halls and the massive lobby without detection, and when I opened the door to the ballroom—it was *empty*. We were so surprised we burst out laughing because no one was there to care. Hotel staff who happened to be cleaning up explained that the projector had broken and the film event had been canceled. I felt bad for the fans, but I think I was more disappointed than anybody, because it would have been such a great surprise. I ended up taking selfies with the staff, and then random fans who caught a glimpse of us on our way back to the rooms also snagged some fun selfies.

The night before we left, Rick Springfield, who in addition to his musical career is famously Dr. Noah Drake on *General Hospital*, appeared at Graceland for a concert in conjunction with the event, and while the fans rocked out in the mosh pit to hits like "Jessie's

Girl," we had a private view of the concert stage-side, which was fun. Finola Hughes, who plays Anna Devane and is a damn great actress, and Laura were dancing up a storm and taking selfies along with other cast members, and after a long day of signing autographs and posing for pictures it was a nice way to relax and let off steam.

Rick also deals with depression and has been open about it publicly. I applaud him for that, because everybody thinks if you're a rock star you've got it made, but this disease can strike anybody, anywhere, in any field, at any given moment. And it does, it just depends on what you do with it.

I was completely caught off guard when shortly after our Graceland excursion I was nominated for an Emmy that year for the work we had done on the Alzheimer's story, but since neither Paula nor I thought I would win, she didn't attend the awards show with me. Instead, we thought it would be fun for Joshua—who had never been to the Emmys—to get dressed up and be my date on the red carpet in Pasadena.

When my category came up, I was still thinking someone else would be going on the stage, because I had been nominated so many times over the past years that I had no expectations. I also still had that peace and calm I had had for months. I know it sounds impossible, but I really couldn't believe it when they called my name. Joshua and Cassidy were also surprised and knew I was totally unprepared, because not only had I not written a speech, I didn't even have a few bullet points scribbled on a notepad and tucked in my jacket to jog my thoughts in a coherent direction.

As I made my way to the stage, there was nothing else to do but speak off the cuff and from the heart, so I reiterated that Alzheimer's was the real star of the story line for educating people, including myself. I thanked my amazing costars and of course advised everyone who was watching that it's probably better to have at least a few notes scribbled on a napkin before getting on a stage.

Even though Paula wasn't there, it meant a lot to have my kids with me and to watch Joshua have that experience for the first time, in the world he's chosen to jump into professionally. Maybe it even makes him think his old man is cool.

When *Victoria Gotti: My Father's Daughter* aired soon after, it immediately began trending and the ratings were great, but although friends and family came to the house and watched it together, I don't like to watch myself on-screen with a crowd and stayed away. It's too nerve-racking, but I was anxious to hear what people thought, so afterward I asked Paula, "Give me the verdict: A, B, C, D, or F?"

She said honestly, "Honey, it's an A-plus." I believed her, because Paula will tell me if it's not. We were watching a rerun of the Desi and Lucy film on TV recently and one of my scenes ended. It was deadly quiet in the room, and not in the good palm-of-my-hand way, and Paula shook her head and said, "Not good, baby."

After everyone left the house, I watched the Gotti film alone. As always, I was critical of my own performance, looking back at scenes I thought were great, and how I could have done them better in different ways. It's sometimes maddening to see which takes filmmakers used and to then try to interpret their choices, but the movie turned out amazing, thanks to all of the talented participants. I even think my accent was pretty good, considering the time I had to prepare. I am very proud to accept the compliment when people tell me I captured Gotti's essence.

Just as I was surprised to win another daytime Emmy for the role of Sonny, I was floored when Lifetime put me up for my first prime-time Emmy for playing John Gotti. In light of the fact that the producer hadn't wanted me in the role, I felt a real sense of accomplishment for breaking into that prime-time awards arena anyway.

Donna would have just loved that; I can hear her laughing now.

Recently I was driving by my old place, where I used to walk Cain, and I started thinking that everything I love in life is either dead, dying, or going to die—and that's just life. As that thought flickered in my head, a guy jumped in front of my car and we locked eyes as I screeched to a stop—just in time. It had suddenly gotten real, and I thought, *It only takes one moment and death takes you.*

The moral of the story—of my story—is to be kind, appreciate your blessings, and love everyone to the fullest. I have so much to appreciate, and among the blessings are healthy parents, a healthy wife, and incredible kids.

Cailey graduated in 2019 with a psychology degree, the first person in my family to matriculate from college. When I walked into the ceremony hall at University of San Diego I was over-whelmed with pride and had to hold it together so I wouldn't break down and take the attention away from my baby girl. As I watched her walk across the stage and receive her diploma, I was struck by what a huge accomplishment it was—and one that was so out of reach for me. It was a phenomenal feeling to watch her top off so many years of hard work. Cailey's always been her own person, de-termined, on a clear path, and I know she'll be a great psychologist. I flashed to her as a little girl chasing snakes, playing princess, and camping out with her little friends in tents to get the first tickets to a Harry Potter movie.

At her graduation party—Harry Potter–themed, of course—she

and her fiancé, Carlos Avila, a paramedic and future firefighter, announced their bridesmaids and groomsmen, including her sisters and brother, presenting them with personalized bobbleheads. He's an incredible guy, and when they got engaged at Disneyland, there was no way for me to escape the ugly-crying. It was that beautiful.

Cailey is in the throes of planning her Belle-inspired wedding, at which I will be giving her away and, on top of that, officiating. I hope I can get through it without losing my composure. Since Paula never got to really fully have her dream wedding, she is enjoying every last detail of planning Cailey's big event with her, and a day doesn't go by that I don't hear Paula and Cailey talking "wedding"!

Heather, on the other hand, was married in June 2019 at the courthouse in San Diego to her longtime boyfriend Philip Andresen, a sergeant in the Marines and a great guy. His family was dressed in cream and ours in splashes of color that Heather picked out for us from the new style department she spearheaded at Macy's San Diego.

It was a sunny California day and Heather was shining just as bright, beautiful in her long, green gown. As I watched her and Philip exchange vows, I remembered her as a little girl—how she ran around with Cailey, let me tease her about everything, the first time she called me Dad. Now, watching her swear her life to someone, my heart was full to bursting. The ceremony was short and simple and Paula and I hosted a dinner for everyone at an Indian restaurant in San Diego.

My youngest daughter, Cassidy, graduated from high school a few years ago, and she is so much like Paula it's no surprise she's her shadow. She helps Paula manage my career, working on everything from booking to appearances. She's a music lover like me, and one of our favorite activities is to hang out and listen to jazz.

Luckily, she isn't accident-prone anymore, but she's still as much of a magnet for animals as Paula, and wants to bring home every cat she sees. She has been dating her boyfriend Anthony Cammarata, who just joined the Air Force, for several years. They are the two quietest people in the world, but you can tell they are deeply in love. It's really wonderful watching that young love play itself out.

It's interesting, all of my girls chose strong, good men with character who serve their country and community. I may do action scenes with explosions or fire or gunshots, but these guys face the real deal. I'm grateful for their service to our country, and am happy they make my girls happy.

My son, Joshua, has also come a long way; whatever he's passionate about, he pursues. This doesn't surprise me because Joshua is good at *everything*, including playing the piano, which he picked up without any lessons. As far as acting goes, there's talent and "magic" talent, and Joshua has the latter in spades. I think he's going to be a movie star. He has already been in his first theater production in Los Angeles, starred in director Spencer Wardwell's American Film Institute film *Boys of a Certain Age*, and is auditioning constantly, all while finishing high school. The fact that girls are already a part of his life blows my mind, because, as with my daughters, I still often see him as a little kid running around getting into things. Sometimes seeing the sensitive, mature man standing before me is a shock.

Seeing all of my children happy and fulfilled is the biggest blessing I could have received. I often thank God I was able to break the cycle of violence of my dad's generation with my own children. Even though I haven't yet broken the pattern of emotional detachment, I am still trying. Now, when everyone's fighting, my skill is being the moderator. I think maybe that's because I'm used to being the one on the outside looking in.

The hard truth of it is that something inside me changed when I went into the mental institution as a young guy. I lost the ability to say, "I love you," to family and friends and girlfriends; it's like a wall went up, and I've been trying to scale it ever since.

Honestly, it's still difficult for me to say, "I love you," unless I'm saying it in character in a scene. The first time I said it to Brenda on *General Hospital*, I was really saying it to Paula. She has always been understanding of that, even though I'm frustrated I can't say, "I love you," to the girls or Joshua the way I wish I could. I do it, but not with the ease that comes so naturally to them with Paula. Although it kills me that Joshua can't say, "I love you," to me, I understand the dynamics and I'm glad at least he can express it to his mom.

Whether or not we actually say those words, though, my kids know I love them, and I know they love me.

I hope someday I'll be able to say, "I love you," and freely offer hugs to the people I love. Donna would kick my butt from heaven if I tried to stop working on that part of me, so I won't. She believed it was possible, and I'm going to try with every breath to prove her right. It pains me that I didn't do it enough with my kids, but all I can do is continue to try, keep working to become a better man.

I do wonder how much of my own journey influenced my children. I wonder if Cailey decided to study psychiatry, with a focus on troubled children, because of everything she knows I have gone through with my mental illness. I wonder if Cassidy is as giving and empathetic as she is, because she's watched Paula reckon with the difficulties of my chemical imbalance and support me no matter what. I wonder if Joshua thinks his father is crazy and never wants to be like me, or if he understands why I am who I am and can relate to me.

It was always amazing to watch the kids with Paula when they were young, because she's such an incredible loving life force, but it has been equally beautiful to watch their relationships change to being close friends as the kids have blossomed into young adults. Paula is so loving and affectionate with them I believe they will be okay, because she's always been my angel—and theirs. Paula also reached her own milestone while I was celebrating my big twenty-five-year achievement, and started a talent agency called Embrace Real Artists. It's the natural next step in a business she's been part of for over twenty-five years. She told me that she wanted to do it to represent the talent that can't find a home, which makes perfect sense, since it's always been her nature to be there for any person (or animal) in need. Of course, her first choice for a junior agent was Cassidy, who is excellent on the computer and incredibly hardworking. She might have just found her passion, too. Together they're a powerhouse, and any talent will be lucky to be represented by ERA.

I have so much to appreciate, so many blessings, and I never would have survived the ups and downs of my illness or achieved what I have in life without my angel, Paula.

After everything in my life, I'm still standing.

The darkness hasn't won.

I'm truly the luckiest man in the world.

CHAPTER SEVENTEEN

Accentuate the Positive

It has been over twenty-seven years since my last breakdown, and I also have not had a lapse on an airplane in several years.

But I do wake up some mornings with that knot in my stomach, that dread for no apparent reason engulfing me, and I still fight the anxiety demon that I will most likely fight the rest of my life. It's a pain in the ass, but I've accepted that's just the way it is. As my father would say, "Lo que pasara pasara."

Now I know I can get through those dark times because I understand I have a choice.

I just have to choose to fight for my life.

I remember how it used to be, fighting in parking lots just to fight, getting into scraps all the time. How far and fast I ran from that mental institution, hoping my demons wouldn't catch up.

When I fight now, it's to save myself. Now I know what my demons are. I've discovered the tools that make up my armor.

I think I'm better at living in the moment, instead of getting trapped inside my head worrying about the next moment (and the next). Something that helped me so much in achieving that state was a book called *The Power of Now* by Eckhart Tolle. The premise—living in the present and being fully present in each moment—makes all the difference in the world. It's the difference between using the day to paint a masterpiece or pulling your hair out.

The meditation technique Dr. Friedemann Schaub taught me has been another invaluable tool. Over the years I have elaborated on it, adding more to the world I visualize when I close my eyes. It's quiet and I take a step, then I take a deep breath, but now I'm walking down a long set of stairs, and as I do, I keep breathing, taking one step at a time in my mind, toward the closed door at the bottom.

When I reach the door, I don't hesitate before opening it. On the other side are a sea of roses and carnations on a huge beautiful green lawn underneath the bluest sky I've ever seen, which is so stunning it's almost blinding to look at. A waterfall is flowing into a large pond on the left, and on the right, far away in the distance, I can see a large building. The architecture is beautiful but I never get inside the building to see what's there, I just know in my deepest soul where I am must be heaven, because it feels like it: full of peace, light, calm, beauty.

I close my eyes and lie down in the flowers and grass. When I open my eyes in this beautiful place, I see Manny, and I'm so elated I hug him. I'm outside of myself watching us talk, but I can't ever hear what we're saying. After a while, something tells me Manny has to go and I walk back through the door and up the stairs.

Sometimes when I leave this meditation I cry because I don't want to say goodbye, but I inevitably feel centered when I open my eyes in the real world again.

Other times, in this meditation, I'm with other people.

Sometimes I'm bringing Paula down the stairs and through the door with me to see her mother. Recently, I went there and found all of my friends who have died too soon, clustered on that beautiful lawn: Jeff, Manny, Carol, Ray, Donna, Corleone, Cain.

It was the most amazing surprise. We were all laughing, and when it was time to go I didn't want to, but I knew I had to, so I hugged everyone goodbye and I went back through the door and up the stairs to my life.

Beyond the visualization, I also have to be diligent and take my medicine, even though I know there's no pill that is a quick fix for everything. That means I also have to take care of myself physically because it's all connected. I eat healthy foods, I don't drink, I work out, box, and go to therapy. If I feel good, all of this makes me feel even better, and if I don't feel great, it helps me maintain equilibrium.

Part of my healthy routine includes sitting in my chair inside the fenced goats' and alpacas' area outside my house and meditating on the view while I drink my coffee. I've also started doing a weekly Instagram video chat on Sundays called *State of Mind* (also available on my website at mbstateofmind.com) while I'm sitting there, talking about what's going on in my mental health journey that week. I'm honest about whether it's going well and whether it's a good week or not, so anyone else out there struggling with a bad week knows they are not alone.

I figure if I'm going through things, other people probably are, too. I have gotten so many responses on social media, it's astounding. A psychiatric nurse recently wrote to me saying she uses me as an example when speaking to her patients, particularly young, newly diagnosed patients who think their lives are over. That makes me so happy. I absolutely love talking to people about overcoming challenges, and now I'm taking that to another level by planning motivational speaking engagements to groups around the country.

It started with Cailey's alma mater, the University of San Diego, which asked me to speak on my mental health journey when Cailey was still a student there. We joined with IBPF to do an event, which Donna's son came to see. I remember Donna saying, years before, he had connected with what I said, and that inspired me to continue educating youth about mental illness.

As I stood in front of all those college students, who were looking forward to their whole lives ahead and their dreams, I realized they were around the age I was when I had first been diagnosed with bipolar disorder. I wondered how many in the sea of strangers were dealing with what I struggled with, not knowing that they were wrestling with a disease that had a name. I wondered if they knew that the first step was letting someone know they needed help.

I wondered if a parent out there had a child who was struggling with it, or if someone's brother or sister or father or mother was dealing with it. I wondered if they knew to look for the signs, and that diagnosis could be elusive like it was for me, but it could be treated with medicine, and managed with therapy.

I wanted to tell them what no one told that little boy I used to see when I looked in the mirror—the little boy who was scared and troubled and ended up in a mental institution. If I could go back and tell that little boy one thing, it would be this: when you're going through hell, you never believe there's going to be light at the end of the tunnel, but the only way out of the tunnel is to keep going through it.

Look at me: I survived the hell.

That younger me who was afraid of his father conquered that fear. The one who saw a mentally challenged kid in class and ached inside because I wanted him to feel joy has reckoned with his own mental illness, and is encouraging others to look in the mirror.

If my story can make a difference in even one other person's life, then it will have made my journey worth it.

Now when I look in the mirror, I see someone who can handle the darkest dark. Someone who can face losing people, can let go of anger, someone who is trying his damnedest to communicate better with his kids, his wife, the people he loves. Someone who isn't afraid to take on adversity as it comes.

I know my journey is far from over, but I also know this—the little boy who was afraid of the dark has found his way to the light.

ACKNOWLEDGMENTS

I am blessed.

You might think it's strange to say that, considering I'm bipolar, but I am, beyond my wildest dreams. I have had so many wonderful opportunities and my life is full of amazing people and love outshines not only the career achievements but the darkness as well. And for all that I am forever grateful.

I am also grateful that there must be angels looking out for me, because I've gone through so much darkness and yet have always survived and always found the light after the low points.

My earthly angel is also the love of my life—I am successful and alive and kicking because of my beautiful wife, Paula. I love you and cherish you more every day and thank God every minute that you didn't get tired of my bullshit. Thank you for going along on what hasn't always been an easy journey and for forgiving all my moods and loving me anyway. You are the best thing that ever happened to me. Aside from your amazing unconditional love, you also gave me the best present I will ever receive, our family, which means more to me than anything else in the world.

ACKNOWLEDGMENTS

To Heather, Cailey, Cassidy, and Joshua, you are my heart, and I love you so much. Being a father has been the highlight of my life even when I don't say that enough. No matter how much success I achieve or how many awards I win, there is no accolade or role or experience that can ever match being your dad. I know you haven't always seen me at my best, but I'm grateful that you still love me and forgive me. You are each so special and make me so proud and I can't wait to see what happens in your lives.

Of course, I wouldn't have my own family if my parents had given up on me when I had my first breakdown. Mom and Dad, I put you through hell, and for that I'm sorry. Mom, you were the first one to really believe in me and I couldn't have gotten to where I am without your love and support. Dad, you're my idol—we may have had our differences, but I'm glad we got to the other side of that and I wouldn't be here if you hadn't helped me out when I was down. I love you both.

This book wouldn't be possible without my entire family letting me share our personal memories with strangers, so I want each of you to know how much I appreciate you understanding the importance of telling my story—the good, bad, and ugly.

Those memories never would have made it to the page if Paula hadn't believed in this book so fiercely, and it would also not be in your hands if she hadn't suggested that our dear friend Susan Black, a fantastic writer, collaborate with me. I really want to thank Sue for being patient with me, asking me the hard questions, and working tirelessly to help make sense of the stories and memories I shared. It was hard and therapeutic for me and Sue understood that, and I can't think of anyone else I could have gone on that journey with. She's the best.

Sue was convinced Jennifer De Chiara was the perfect agent

for the book, and she couldn't have been more correct. Jennifer, your instincts were invaluable and I want to thank you for that and for bringing the amazing team at HarperCollins on board. Thank you to our insightful editor Anna Montague, Lisa Sharkey and her Creative Development team, Benjamin Steinberg and the marketing team, Kelly Rudolph and the publicity team, and Jim Warren for the kick-ass cover photo.

I'm fortunate that I have had such good friends to share my life with and even though some are gone, I carry a piece of them in my heart and head and they have also made me who I am. Jeff, Ray, Manny, Carol, Donna, and all my animals, thank you for everything and I'll see you in my dreams. To the friends who are still around, thanks for still putting up with me. Melissa Heck, thank you for always being there to help me through my really tough times and understanding who I really am and believing in me from the moment we met. Thanks, too, for always being there to help Paula and the family. There are too many things to list, but I appreciate all of it more than you know. I'm glad you're in my world—and really glad you relentlessly bugged me to do that social media thing.

I don't know where I'd be without the acting teachers who took an interest when I was green. Many thanks to Howard Fine for showing me what acting is all about, Alan Drew for being my early mentor, and Joan Kenley for changing my voice and helping change my career.

I've worked with so many great actors. I love actors, and to all my costars both on *GH* and the films I've worked in, you don't realize how much you all mean to mean to me and how much I learned from everyone. Angelo Pagán, thanks for letting me take your place in the play, Michael Knight for being so funny, Desi

Arnaz for being a great character to play, and Frances Fisher for being so kind to a young and scared actor.

To the rest of my *GH* family: Thank you first and foremost to Wendy Riche and Shelley Curtis for giving me the opportunity of a lifetime and sticking with me when I had a breakdown. Bob Guza, thanks for the Dark Side, Jill Farren-Phelps for being the mother I needed at work during rough periods, and the crew, you're awesome—Dean Cosanella, my cameraman with beautiful hair; Jerry O'Dwyer, the Santa Claus of the crew; Craiger—Craig McManus—one of the kindest men I know and who Donna loved dearly; Anzhela Adzhiya, who makes my hair look perfect every day; Nneka Garland, thanks for being Nneka; and everyone else on the crew, you mean more to me than you know. Our multi-Emmy-Award-winning casting director, Mark Teschner, thanks for surrounding me with amazing talent for twenty-seven years. And last but not least, Frank Valentini, the master at keeping the machine running, you just know what's needed and somehow make it happen. It blows me away how generous you have always been, just saying, "Spread your wings," whenever I wanted and needed to do other projects creatively.

Part of that *GH* family includes all of you out there who have cared and tuned in over the years. I can't thank you enough and I wish I could really tell you how incredible, honored, and privileged it has made me feel that you have believed in me from the start. Your loyalty to *GH* is second to none and your loyalty to me leaves me speechless.

There are many professionals who have helped me on my mental health journey and I really owe them my gratitude. First and foremost, Dr. Noonan, you saved my life. Holly Hines, thank you for supporting me in times of real crisis. Dr. Friedemann

ACKNOWLEDGMENTS

Schaub, you are the most incredible therapist for my struggle with anxiety and have helped me tremendously.

Oprah, Dr. Drew, and Dr. Oz also deserve a huge shout-out for letting me use their wonderful public platforms for mental health education. Oprah, thank you for being Oprah and for allowing me to open up about really dark events. You were so incredible to me and my wife and I'll never forget it. Dr. Oz, thank you for giving me the opportunity to speak in depth about my bipolar experience. Dr. Drew, I'm glad we have a connection—your insight is uncanny.

To the National Alliance on Mental Illness (NAMI), Didi Hirsch Mental Health Services, the Depression and Bipolar Support Alliance (DBSA), the International Bipolar Foundation (IBPF), and all the other mental health organizations I have had the honor to be associated with, you rock for the important work you do.

To all the people, famous or not, who are brave enough to get up every day and keep on facing challenges, and to share their mental health stories with others, thank you. To every person out there who had the courage to write me or tell me in person about their pain and said I helped them or inspired them by telling my story, that humbles and moves me more than you know and you also inspired *me* to put everything down in this book.

For anyone who may be having a tough time, reach out and talk to somebody about it. It helps. Hang on to hope and hang in there—the darkness doesn't last forever and the light will reappear. It isn't always easy but it's possible; I'm proof of that.

As Paula always says, "You're stronger than you know."

MAURICE BENARD is a two-time Emmy Award–winning film and television actor, a member of the prestigious Actors Studio, and an advocate for mental health awareness. Diagnosed with bipolar disorder at age twenty-two, he has since worked with numerous organizations to raise awareness, and has been honored many times over the years by the International Bipolar Foundation, the National Alliance of Mental Illness, Mental Health America, and Didi Hirsch Mental Health Services, to name a few. He is passionate about erasing the stigma surrounding mental health and reaching out to those in need by speaking at events and on his weekly Instagram program *State of Mind*, as well as launching the website mbstateofmind.com. Early on in his career he played Desi Arnaz, and more recently John Gotti, in their popular biopics. He lives in California with his wife, Paula, numerous animals, and is the proud father of three daughters and a son.

SUSAN BLACK'S screenwriting credits include NBC's Emmy Award–winning series *A Year in the Life*; HBO's *State of Emergency*, for which she received the PEN Literary Award and CableAce and Humanitas Award nominations; and Showtime's *Tapestries of Hope*, shot in Zimbabwe, which she also produced, to name a few. Previously a staff writer at Warner Bros. Pictures, Black is also an alumnus of the American Film Institute Conservatory drama program and resides in California with her animals. She currently has several projects in development and is working on her next book.

IF YOU or someone you know needs help, here is the contact information for several organizations I've been involved with that have been helpful to me and many others. Their websites offer invaluable information and you can also call or text them for immediate assistance or simply for more information. Don't be afraid to reach out to someone; if not these organizations, please talk to a medical professional, clergy member, loved one, or friend. Just don't try to go it alone.

In the event of a crisis, go to an emergency room, or, in the US, call 9-1-1 or The National Suicide Prevention Lifeline. It is open 24/7 and the phone number is 800-273-TALK (8255). For a list of international hotlines click on your country at www.suicide.org.

INTERNATIONAL BIPOLAR FOUNDATION
www.ibpf.org
TEXT: Text START to 741-741.

NATIONAL ALLIANCE ON MENTAL ILLNESS (NAMI)
www.nami.org
TEXT: Text NAMI to 741-741.

DEPRESSION AND BIPOLAR SUPPORT ALLIANCE
www.dbsalliance.org
TEXT: Text DBSA to 741-741.

DIDI HIRSCH MENTAL HEALTH SERVICES

https://didihirsch.org/

TEXT: text HEARME to 839863.

OTHER HOTLINES:

Self-harm Hotline (1-800-366-8288; www.selfinjury.com)

The Friendship Line (1-800-971-0016; www.ioaging.org)

Covenant House (The 9 Line: 1-800-999-9999; www.covenanthouse.org)

7 Cups of Tea (www.7cups.com)